Bitesize
Pearson Edexcel
GCSE (9-1)
GEOGRAPHY B
REVISION GUIDE

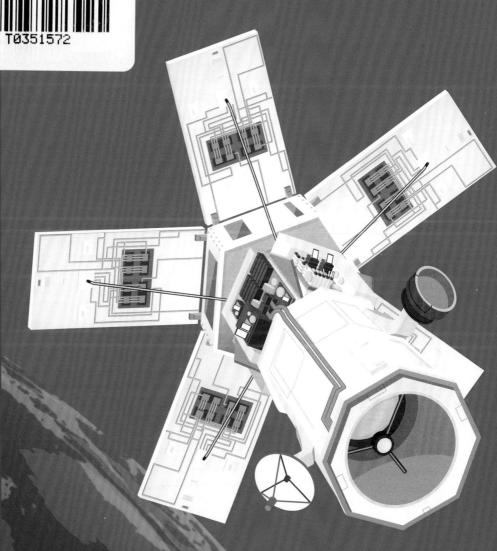

Series Consultant:
Harry Smith

Author:
Rob Bircher

Contents

✓ Tick off each topic as you go.

② Each bite-sized chunk has a **timer** to indicate how long it will take. Use them to plan your revision sessions.

 Scan the **QR codes** to visit the BBC Bitesize website. It will link straight through to revision resources on that subject. You can also access these by visiting www.pearsonschools. co.uk/BBCBitesizeLinks.

Grades have been assigned to most questions in this Revision Guide. These are intended to show you the level of challenge of those questions, and to help you track your progress. In your exam, your grade will be based on your overall mark, and not on your responses to individual questions.

How to use this book

Use the features in this book to focus your revision, track your progress through the topics and practise your exam skills.

 Features to help you revise

Scan the **QR codes** to visit the BBC Bitesize website. It will link straight through to more revision resources on that subject.

Each bite-sized chunk has a **timer** to indicate how long it will take. Use them to plan your revision sessions.

Topics that are related to **geographical skills** are explained in callouts and in the Geographical skills section at the back.

Complete **worked examples** demonstrate how to approach exam-style questions.

Test yourself with exam-style practice at the end of each page and check your answers at the back of the book.

Tick boxes allow you to track the sections you have revised. Revisit each page to embed your knowledge.

[Sample page shown: "Development" — Global geographical issues / Development dynamics. Sections include Economic measures – advantages and disadvantages, Social measures of development, Measures of inequality, Geographical skills, Worked example (Grades 5–7), Figure 1 Map showing countries by their HDI score, Exam-style practice (Grades 4–5). Page 17.]

 **Exam focus features**

The *About your exam* section at the start of the book gives you all the key information about your exams, as well as showing you how to identify the different questions.

Throughout the topic pages you will also find green *Exam skills* pages. These pages work through an extended exam-style question and provide further opportunities to practise your skills.

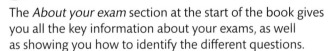 **ActiveBook and app**

This Revision Guide comes with a **free online edition**. Follow the instructions inside the front cover to access your ActiveBook.

You can also download the **free BBC Bitesize app** to access revision flash cards and quizzes.

If you do not have a QR code scanner, you can access all the links in this book from your ActiveBook or visit **www.pearsonschools.co.uk/BBCBitesizeLinks**.

[Sample page shown: "Making a geographical decision" and "Four-mark questions" — About your exam. Page vii and 87.]

Your Geography GCSE

This page will tell you everything you need to know about the structure of your upcoming Edexcel GCSE Geography B exam.

 About the exam papers

You will have to take **three papers** as part of your Edexcel GCSE Geography B qualification. The papers will test your knowledge, understanding and geographical skills. Each of the papers has a different focus. Paper 1 is all about global geographical issues and Paper 2 is all about UK geographical issues. Paper 3 has four sections, and focuses on making a geographical decision, drawing on your knowledge of people and environment issues and global, as well as UK geographical issues. There are some optional topics in Paper 1 and Paper 2.

Paper 1
Global geographical issues
1 hour 30 minutes
94 marks in total

Paper 2
UK geographical issues
1 hour 30 minutes
94 marks in total

Paper 3
People and environment issues – making geographical decisions
1 hour 30 minutes
64 marks in total

 Papers 1 and 2

Papers 1 and 2 have three sections: A, B and C.
In Paper 1, you will be examined on these topics:

- Hazardous Earth
- Development dynamics
- Challenges of an urbanising world.

In Paper 2, you will be examined on these topics:

- The UK's evolving physical landscape
- The UK's evolving human landscape
- Geographical investigations.

In Paper 2, Section C, you will need to answer **one** question on a physical fieldwork investigation and **one** question on a human fieldwork investigation.

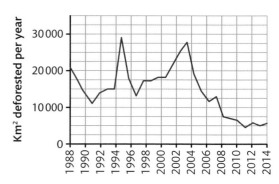

 Paper 3: People and environment issues – making geographical decisions

The third paper is different from Papers 1 and 2. In the exam, you will be given a booklet of sources to analyse and interpret. In the final 12-mark question, you will need to make and justify a geographical decision using information from the booklet of sources and your own knowledge of physical and human geography from throughout your course.

Sections A, B and C

In Section A you will be examined on People and the biosphere; in Section B you will be examined on Forests under threat, and in Section C you will be examined on Consuming energy resources. Section C includes 8-mark extended writing questions.

Section D: Making a geographical decision

This section consists of one extended writing question worth 12 marks, plus 4 marks for spelling, punctuation, grammar and your use of specialist terminology, for a total of 16 marks. You will be given three options for a decision related to the sources in the Resource Booklet. You will need to choose one option and justify your choice in your answer. You should use information from the Resource Booklet, and the knowledge and understanding you have gained throughout your GCSE Geography course.

Multiple-choice questions

Multiple-choice questions give you several options to choose from. You must indicate the correct answer by marking your choice clearly.

⑤ Exam explainer

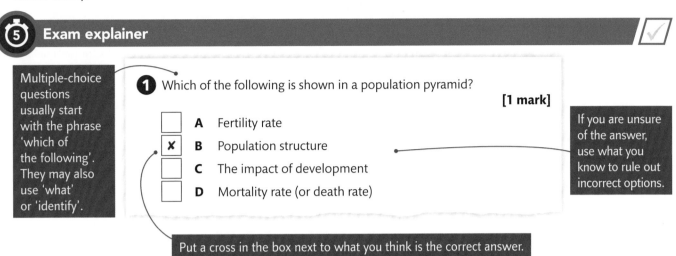

Multiple-choice questions usually start with the phrase 'which of the following'. They may also use 'what' or 'identify'.

1 Which of the following is shown in a population pyramid?

[1 mark]

☐ **A** Fertility rate
☒ **B** Population structure
☐ **C** The impact of development
☐ **D** Mortality rate (or death rate)

If you are unsure of the answer, use what you know to rule out incorrect options.

Put a cross in the box next to what you think is the correct answer.

Some questions require you to engage with a map, graph or photo. Look at the figure carefully and make sure you understand what it is showing before you answer the question.

Figure 1 This type of work can involve long hours and low pay.

Study **Figure 1**, which shows a worker in a textile factory. Identify which economic sector is shown.

☐ **A** Primary sector
☒ **B** Secondary sector
☒ **C** Tertiary sector
☐ **D** Quaternary sector

If you want to change your answer, put a line through the box and then mark your new answer with a cross.

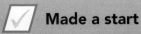

Short-answer questions

Short-answer questions come in a variety of forms and are the most common type of questions. They are worth 1–3 marks.

(2) Command words

- ☑ **calculate** – give a numerical answer and show your working
- ☑ **name** – produce an answer from memory
- ☑ **identify** – name or characterise
- ☑ **state** – express in clear terms
- ☑ **define** – give the meaning of a term
- ☑ **describe** – set out characteristics

- ☑ **explain** – set out purposes or reasons for how or why something happens
- ☑ **label** – add a label to a resource or image
- ☑ **draw** – create a visual representation of information
- ☑ **compare** – find similarities and differences between two things
- ☑ **suggest** – provide a reasoned explanation for something

(2) Exam focus

Short-answer questions should be quick to complete, so you should aim to spend a few minutes on each one.

(10) Exam explainer

Make sure you read the question carefully so you know how many points to include in your answer – this question asks for two factors.

1 Identify **one** reason why tropical storms lose their energy.

[1 mark]

This type of 1-mark question only needs a short answer.

2 Identify **two** reasons why secondary employment has decreased in the UK.

[2 marks]

Many short-answer questions use images. Check that you are using the correct figure and look at it carefully.

3

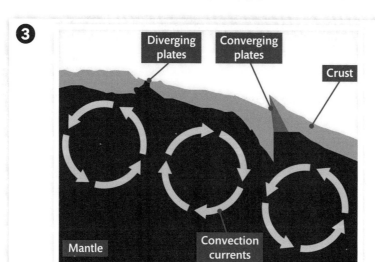

Figure 2 Convection currents in the Earth's mantle cause tectonic plate movement.

Study **Figure 2**, which shows convection currents in the Earth's mantle. Explain how convection moves the Earth's tectonic plates. **[3 marks]**

Some **describe**, **explain**, **suggest**, **draw** and **compare** questions are worth 3 marks and require more detail. Look at the number of marks available for a question to tell you how much detail you need to provide in your answer – the more marks available, the more detailed your answer should be.

 Made a start   **Feeling confident**   **Exam ready**

Four-mark questions

Four-mark questions are a very common exam question type. They use the command words **explain** and **suggest**.

 Exam explainer

For four-mark questions, you need to make two clear points and develop each one with an explanation or justification.

You could be asked to study a resource, such as a map, graph, photo, table or sketch drawing, in any of your exams. For this type of question, it is important you carefully look at the resource provided so you understand exactly what it is showing before you begin to write your answer.

1 Analyse **Figure 1**, which shows the distribution of earthquakes and volcanoes in relation to plate boundaries.

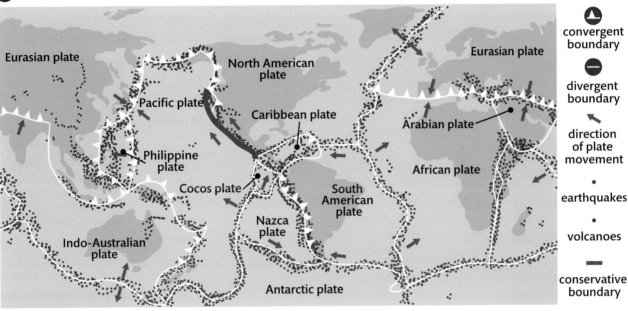

Figure 1 The distribution of earthquakes and volcanoes

Suggest **two** reasons for the distribution of earthquakes in **Figure 1**.

[4 marks]

Include specific details from the map in your answer, such as the names of tectonic plates.

2 Explain why the fertility rate varies between countries. [4 marks]

If you are asked to **explain**, refer to specific features and develop your points by giving reasons. Use specialist terminology accurately to show your knowledge.

 **Command words**

- ☑ **suggest** – provide a reasoned explanation
- ☑ **explain** – set out purposes or reasons for how or why something happens

 **Structure your answers**

- ☑ Make a **point** – for example: *Deforestation can lead to the loss of biodiversity in rainforests.*
- ☑ **Develop** your point – for example: *This is because it destroys the natural habitat of many plant and animal species so they can no longer live there.*
- ☑ **Link** your point back to the question – for example: *This reduces biodiversity because there will be a loss of plant and animal species.*

Extended-response questions

Some questions require you to write a longer answer that demonstrates your knowledge and understanding of Geography and your ability to develop ideas in a structured way.

② Command words ☑

- ☑ **assess** – use evidence to decide the significance of something, considering all factors
- ☑ **evaluate** – make a judgement using evidence
- ☑ **justify** – support a decision or opinion using evidence

② Exam focus ☑

One extended response question in each paper includes 4 marks for accuracy of spelling, punctuation, grammar (SPaG) and specialist terminology.

Aim to spend 10–15 minutes answering this question, including time for checking your work.

㉂ Exam explainer ☑

This **evaluate** question requires you to look critically at your fieldwork investigation, and make a judgement about how important secondary data was. Back up your statements with evidence.

1 For a named megacity, assess how far rapid economic growth has affected attempts to improve quality of life.

[8 marks]

Include detailed information about one of the case studies you have learned about. You need to use evidence to make a judgement – in this case the impact of economic growth on improving quality of life.

2 Evaluate the importance of secondary data in your investigation.

[8 marks]

For an **evaluate** question you need to include a definite judgement or conclusion.

In this question, 4 of the marks awarded will be for your spelling, punctuation and grammar and your use of specialist terminology.

3 Assess the reasons why earthquake preparation is usually more effective in developed countries than in developing countries.

[12 marks]

In Paper 1 and Paper 2 you might be asked a 12-mark question, where 4 of the marks are awarded for spelling, punctuation, grammar and specialist terminology.

In a **justify** question, you will be given three options. Choose one, but demonstrate that you have considered all the options and give reasons for not choosing the others.

In this question, 4 of the marks awarded will be for your spelling, punctuation and grammar and your use of specialist terminology.

4 Select the option that you think would be the best **long-term** plan for how Britain's energy should be generated in the future. Justify your choice.

Use information from the Resource Booklet and knowledge and understanding from the rest of your geography course to support your answer.

[16 marks]

The 16-mark question appears at the end of Paper 3.

☑ **Made a start**   ☑ **Feeling confident**   ☑ **Exam ready**

General atmospheric circulation

The Earth's atmosphere is constantly moving. It transfers heat energy from one location to another via atmospheric circulation cells.

⑩ Circulation cells

Solar radiation is spread over a wider area of distribution at the poles than at the equator. In both hemispheres, the redistribution of heat energy is caused by three atmospheric circulation cells: the Hadley cell, the Ferrel cell and the Polar cell. Heat energy is transferred where the cells meet.

1 Warmed air rises at the equator, causing low pressure. The air moves north and south and cools to create **Hadley cells**. At latitudes of 30° north and south, the cooled air sinks, causing high pressure.

2 Some cooled air flows back towards the equator as surface **trade winds**. The rest of the air moves towards the poles, forming part of the **Ferrel cells**.

3 At latitudes of 60° north and south, the warmer air of the Ferrel cells meets colder polar air at the polar fronts. A polar jet stream is formed above this, which drives the unstable atmosphere. The warmer air rises to form **Polar cells**. This air travels north or south to the poles, where it cools and sinks, forming areas of high pressure.

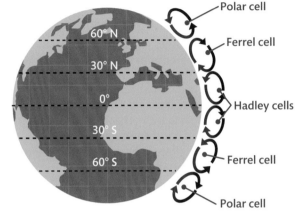

Figure 1 Heat energy flow in a circulation cell

⑤ Ocean currents

Currents in the ocean also redistribute heat energy around the globe.

1 At the poles (in the Arctic and Antarctic), the water in the sea gets very cold. This cold water sinks down towards the bottom of the sea.

2 Away from the poles, the sea is warmer because solar radiation (heat energy from the Sun) is more intense.

3 As the cold water sinks at the poles, warmer water from lower latitudes is pulled in to replace it, creating a current.

4 When the warmer water reaches the poles, it cools and sinks and the process continues.

⑤ Worked example — Grades 5–7

Study **Figure 1**, which shows circulation cells in the global atmospheric circulation system.

Explain how global atmospheric circulation determines the location of arid (high pressure) and high rainfall (low pressure) areas. **[4 marks]**

At the equator, the Sun's heat energy is most intense. Warm, moist air rises, creating areas of very low pressure with very heavy rainfall. The air then travels north and south to about 30° north and south of the equator, cooling on the way. As it cools it sinks, creating high pressure. Because the air is dry in these areas of high pressure, clouds and rain do not form, making these areas arid, with less than 200 mm of precipitation per year.

② Exam-style practice — Grades 5–6

Identify the global atmospheric circulation cell located between 30° latitude and the equator. **[1 mark]**

☐ **A** Hadley cell
☐ **B** Ferrel cell
☐ **C** Polar cell
☐ **D** Trade wind

Causes of climate change

Most climate scientists agree that the main cause of global warming is the **greenhouse effect**, which is accelerated by human activity. However, there are also some natural causes that contribute towards climate change.

 Natural causes of climate change

Orbital changes

Milutin Milanković, a geophysicist and astronomer, believed that changes in the Earth's orbit resulted in cyclical variation in the solar radiation reaching the Earth (Milankovitch cycles).

1 **Eccentricity** – The Earth's orbit changes from elliptical (warmer periods) to less elliptical (cooler periods) approximately every 100 000 years.

2 **Axial tilt** – The Earth's tilt on its axis varies between 22.1° and 24.5° over a period of 41 000 years. A larger tilt leads to more extreme seasons, such as warmer summers.

3 **Precession** – Sometimes, the Earth wobbles while spinning, which can affect the severity of the seasons in one hemisphere compared with the other.

Volcanic activity

Volcanic eruptions cause large amounts of sulphur dioxide gas and ash to be released into the atmosphere.
The sulphur dioxide reacts with other substances to produce sulphate particles, which reflect nearly all radiation, reducing the amount of solar radiation entering the Earth's atmosphere and so causing global cooling. However, volcanic activity can also have the opposite effect; the release of the greenhouse gas carbon dioxide (CO_2) during periods of extreme volcanic activity has caused global warming.

Solar output

Some scientists believe that solar radiation may be a significant cause of increasing global temperatures. However, satellite measurements of solar output since 1978 actually show a slight drop in solar irradiance. Most analysis of longer-term sunspot records indicates that it is unlikely that a change in solar irradiance is the main reason for recent warming.

 The greenhouse effect

When heat from the Sun is radiated to the Earth, some of it is trapped in the Earth's atmosphere by greenhouse gases, such as water vapour, carbon dioxide and methane, and some of it is reflected back into space. Greenhouse gases maintain the temperature of the Earth making it a habitable environment. As the concentration of greenhouse gases is increasing, more heat is becoming trapped in the Earth's atmosphere, so the temperature of the Earth is rising. This is the enhanced greenhouse effect.

 Worked example   **Grade 5**

Explain why asteroid collisions caused climate change.
[4 marks]

When asteroids hit the Earth in the past, the impacts threw huge amounts of debris, smoke and dust into the atmosphere, some of which reached high altitudes and spread out. These vast clouds of smoke and dust blocked the Sun's heat and light from reaching the Earth. This changed the climate and cooled the planet.

 Human causes of climate change

Energy

Burning fossil fuels, such as coal and oil, leads to an increased release of CO_2 into the atmosphere. A higher concentration of CO_2 in the atmosphere will enhance the greenhouse effect.

Industry

Industry is also a major source of greenhouse gases, including nitrous oxide and fluorinated gases, which have a much stronger warming effect than CO_2. Cement production is one of the biggest industrial emitters of greenhouse gases.

Farming

The farming of livestock, such as cows, produces methane gas, as do the cultivation methods of crops such as rice. Like CO_2, methane is a greenhouse gas and a key contributor towards the greenhouse effect.

Transport

Most fuel is petroleum-based. This means burning fuels for cars, planes, ships and other transport vehicles generates large amounts of greenhouse gases, particularly CO_2.

 Exam-style practice   **Grades 1–3**

Suggest **one** human cause of climate change.
[2 marks]

 Made a start   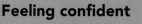 **Feeling confident**   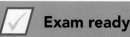 **Exam ready**

Climate change evidence

Since the start of the Quaternary period, almost 2.6 million years ago, there have been several cycles of glacial advance and retreat. The end of the last Ice Age was about 11 500 years ago.

(5) Changing global temperatures

Figure 1 shows how the annual global temperature is increasing and provides evidence for **climate change** (commonly known as **global warming**). The year 2010 was the warmest year globally since records began in 1880 and some scientists predict that temperatures will continue to rise rapidly. In 2010, the annual global combined land and ocean surface temperature was 0.94 °C above the 20th century average. This was the 39th consecutive year (since 1977) that the yearly global temperature was above average.

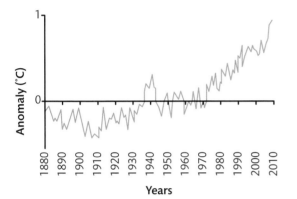

Figure 1 Annual global temperature anomalies from 1880–2010 relative to the 20th-century average (shown by the horizontal axis, at 0)

(5) Evidence of human causes

Rising sea levels

In the 20th century, global sea levels rose by about 14 cm. They are rising faster now than they were 50 years ago. The world's oceans are warming up, with a 0.1 °C rise in the last century. Data models show that the rate at which sea levels rise will increase in the future as Arctic ice sheets melt.

Glacial retreat

Long-term data trends show that glaciers are retreating at a historically unprecedented rate. The ice in the Himalayas, the Andes, the Alps and the Rockies is retreating at ever greater speeds.

Declining ice

Recent NASA data has shown a decrease in the size of the ice sheets in Greenland and Antarctica. The extent and thickness of Arctic sea ice has been rapidly declining in recent decades. Monthly September ice extent for 1979 to 2016 declined by 13.2 per cent per decade.

Increased likelihood of extreme weather events

The number of extreme weather events around the world has increased in recent years. Different scientific studies have used computer modelling to make links between the contribution of human activity to rising global temperatures and the likelihood of extreme weather events occurring.

(5) Evidence of natural causes

Ice cores and tree rings can provide more evidence for how the Earth's climate has changed over time.

Ice cores can provide information about what the climate was like hundreds of thousands of years ago. Scientists use these to determine what the climate was like during glacial and interglacial periods and how it has changed from Roman times to the present day.

Obtained from drilling deep into ice sheets, ice cores contain bubbles of air from when the ice was formed. These bubbles can be sampled to determine the levels of greenhouse gases in the atmosphere at that time.

Tree rings tend to grow wider in warm, wet years and narrower in cold, dry years. By compiling tree ring data, scientists can gather evidence about how the climate has changed over hundreds of years.

(5) Worked example   Grade 4

Suggest **two** ways the consequences of climate change may affect people.   [4 marks]

Rising sea levels are likely to increase coastal flooding, and could make many coastal areas around the world uninhabitable. An increase in global temperatures is likely to change which crops can be grown in which countries, and may make food supply more insecure.

(5) Exam-style practice   Grade 5

Many scientists believe our climate is changing. Describe the evidence for climate change.   [3 marks]

Predicting climate change

There is a range of projections for future increases in global temperatures and sea level rise. There are too many uncertainties to make precise predictions about the effects that climate change will have.

⑩ Uncertain climate projections

Scientists use computer models to make predictions about climate change. They input huge amounts of data, including past temperature and sea level records, data obtained from ice cores and satellite observation data, in order to make predictions about global temperatures and sea levels in the future. The models can be adjusted to predict how the climate may change in different scenarios, for example if greenhouse gas emissions continue to rise, remain at current levels or are significantly reduced. However, there are many variables, and the oceans and the atmosphere are extremely complex. This means it is impossible to predict with certainty how much global temperatures will change and sea levels will rise.

Global temperature predictions

Most scientific research predicts an average global temperature increase of between 1.5 °C and 4.5 °C over the next century. However, some models have found that increases of up to 6 °C may be possible – far beyond the 2 °C increase above pre-industrial levels that is considered dangerous under the Paris Agreement (2016).

Global sea level rise predictions

The speed at which sea levels are rising has increased. The average sea level rise in the 20th century was between 1.1 mm and 1.7 mm per year, but it is now 3.1 mm per year. Predictions published by the US National Oceanic and Atmospheric Administration (NOAA) for the amount of sea level rise between 2000 and 2100 range from 0.3 m to 2.5 m.

Reasons for uncertainty

- The atmosphere and oceans are extremely complex and may respond to changes in unexpected ways.
- It is not certain what the extent of Arctic and Antarctic ice sheet loss will be.
- There is uncertainty about future changes in cloud cover and its effect on global warming.
- The rate of future greenhouse gas emissions is difficult to predict.

⑤ Key facts

- Increased temperatures could see a rise in extreme weather events such as droughts and flooding, causing significant impacts on freshwater environments and the lives of people who live there.
- An average increase of 1.5 °C could see a 20–30 per cent increase of species at risk of extinction worldwide.
- Rising sea levels could threaten the lives of people living in low-lying coastal areas in, for example, Bangladesh and the Maldives.
- Rising temperatures are likely to cause drought, which will increase the pressure upon water resources.
- Rising sea temperatures are increasing the bleaching of coral reefs, with scientists predicting that, by 2050, 98 per cent of reefs around the world will be affected.

Figure 1 Rising sea temperatures have caused coral bleaching in the Caribbean Sea.

② Exam-style practice   Grade 3

Suggest **one** reason for uncertainty about climate change projections.   **[2 marks]**

 Made a start   **Feeling confident**   **Exam ready**

Distribution of tropical cyclones

Tropical cyclones are also known as **hurricanes** or **typhoons**, depending on where they develop in the world. You need to know how, where and when they occur.

⑩ Global distribution of tropical storms

Tropical cyclones only affect some countries, because they require certain conditions to form. They form in the tropics between approximately 5° and 30° latitude (between the Tropic of Cancer and the Tropic of Capricorn, but not normally at the equator). They tend to occur in the northern tropics between June and November, and in the southern tropics between November and April. Tropical cyclones are given different names depending on where they occur in the world:

- **hurricanes** have their source area in the Atlantic Ocean
- **typhoons** have their source area in the north-west Pacific Ocean
- **cyclones** have their source area in the South Pacific or the Indian Ocean.

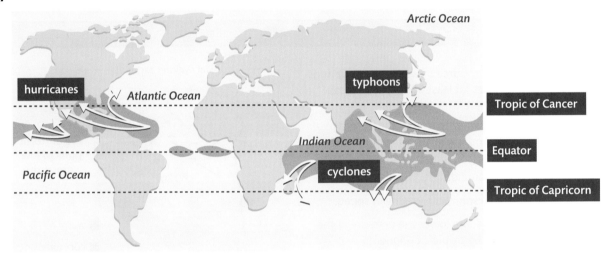

Figure 1 Global distribution and movement of tropical cyclones – the arrows show that they tend to track (move) westwards, because they are affected by the prevailing trade winds.

⑤ Conditions needed

- ☑ Warm sea temperatures – at least 26.5 °C at the sea's surface
- ☑ A lot of water vapour in the atmosphere
- ☑ Low pressure disturbances and smaller storms that can join to form a tropical cyclone
- ☑ Rapidly cooling water vapour, which forms cumulonimbus clouds
- ☑ Warm air rising from the ocean, which is pulled into a column of clouds
- ☑ Coriolis effect creates spinning of the rising column of air. (The coriolis effect does not create tropical cyclones within 5° of the equator.)

② Worked example — Grades 1–2

Study **Figure 1**, which shows the source areas and tracks of tropical cyclones.

Which of the following best describes the tracks of tropical cyclones? **[1 mark]**

- ☒ **A** Hurricanes can form in the Atlantic Ocean and travel west.
- ☐ **B** Cyclones can form in the Pacific Ocean and travel east.
- ☐ **C** Cyclones can form in the Indian Ocean and travel north.
- ☐ **D** Typhoons can form in the Pacific Ocean and travel east.

① Exam focus

Before your exam, make sure you know the location of the seven continents and the five major oceans.

② Exam-style practice — Grades 1–2

State **one** factor that influences the distribution of tropical cyclones. **[1 mark]**

Causes and hazards of tropical cyclones

The term **tropical cyclone** refers to the low pressure systems that form over tropical or subtropical waters.

⏱ 5 Key features of tropical cyclones

- ☑ Tropical cyclones create areas of very low pressure, high winds, and heavy rainfall.
- ☑ They form a cylinder of rising, spiralling air (Coriolis effect) surrounding an **eye** of descending cool air.
- ☑ The eye of the storm is a region of clear skies where cool air is descending.
- ☑ Cloud banks known as the **eye wall** surround the eye. The strongest winds tend to occur in the eye wall.
- ☑ Tropical cyclones **intensify** when there is high humidity. They **dissipate** when they move into areas of colder water, hit land or meet winds blowing in different directions.

⏱ 10 Formation of a tropical cyclone

1 Tropical cyclones require a source of warm, moist air and warm ocean temperatures (at least 26.5 °C at the sea's surface). This restricts where they can form.

2 The warm ocean causes water to evaporate, forming cumulonimbus clouds, and warm air rising rapidly from the ocean causes thunderstorms.

3 These converge, and an area of very low pressure forms.

4 As the air rises it starts to spin, accelerating in speed.

5 The faster the wind speed, the lower the pressure at the centre and the stronger the tropical cyclone.

6 The rising air cools and condenses and more cumulonimbus clouds form and grow, bringing rain, thunder and lightning.

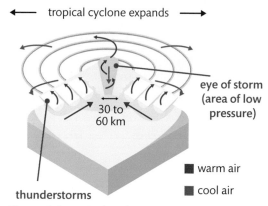

← tropical cyclone expands →

eye of storm (area of low pressure)

30 to 60 km

■ warm air
■ cool air

thunderstorms

Figure 1 A tropical cyclone

⏱ 5 Tropical cyclone hazards

- **Wind speeds** exceed 119 km per hour and can reach 250 km per hour or more. The strongest winds can damage or destroy buildings.
- The very low pressure of a tropical cyclone causes the sea to bulge upwards, while winds blow the water towards the coast. These **storm surges** can be many metres high and can cause loss of life and devastating damage to buildings and the environment.

- **Intense rainfall** can cause flooding.
- Higher sea levels can cause **coastal flooding**. Salt water can ruin crops.
- Intense rainfall can saturate slopes and cause **landslides**. These can happen miles from the coast as intense rain moves inland from the sea.

⏱ 2 Worked example — Grades 3–4 ☑

Suggest **two** characteristics of a tropical cyclone. ◄
[2 marks]

Characteristics of a tropical cyclone means features of a tropical cyclone.

One characteristic of a tropical cyclone is that it is an area of very low pressure. A second characteristic is that it has an eye wall that surrounds the eye.

⏱ 5 Exam-style practice — Grade 5 ☑

Explain how tropical cyclones are formed. **[4 marks]**

☑ **Made a start**　　☑ **Feeling confident**　　☑ **Exam ready**

Impacts of tropical cyclones

Some countries are more vulnerable than others to the impacts of tropical cyclones. Physical, social and economic factors affect a country's vulnerability.

⑤ Physical vulnerability

Physical factors can make countries more vulnerable to the impacts of tropical cyclones.

- Countries with low-lying coastal areas are vulnerable to high winds and storm surges. Low-lying countries such as Bangladesh and island nations such as the Philippines are especially vulnerable.
- Some coastlines, such as the coastline around the Bay of Bengal, have a funnel shape that increases wind speeds and the height of storm surges.
- Storm surges are more intense when the ocean floor is a gentle, gradual slope. A steeply sloping ocean floor can reduce the size of storm surges.

Figure 1 The funnel shape of the Bay of Bengal makes Bangladesh and Myanmar more vulnerable to the impacts of tropical cyclones.

⑤ Social vulnerability

- Buildings in poorer countries may be made out of weaker materials and may be less well constructed, making them vulnerable to cyclone damage.
- In vulnerable areas, richer people often live on higher ground while poorer people live in the areas most at risk of coastal flooding.
- Developing countries, or poorer areas within a developed country, may not have efficient transport to help people evacuate. This was one reason for more than 1830 people dying in the USA in 2005, during Hurricane Katrina.
- Countries with a very high population density, such as Bangladesh, are more vulnerable to the impacts of tropical cyclones.

⑤ Worked example   Grade 6

Analyse **Figure 2**, which shows the location of the five most deadly tropical cyclones in the last 100 years.

Year	Location	Number of deaths
1970	Bangladesh	300 000–500 000
1975	China	approximately 150 000
1991	Bangladesh	138 866
2008	Myanmar	138 366
1922	China	60 000–100 000

Figure 2

Suggest **two** reasons why the five most deadly cyclones were all in developing or emerging countries.   **[4 marks]**

One reason could be economic: these developing and emerging countries probably did not have accurate monitoring or prediction technology at the time of the tropical cyclones, so they would not have been able to evacuate people from areas that were at risk.

Another reason could be social: the people who died may have been living in densely populated, low-lying coastal regions that were hit by storm surges.

⑤ Economic vulnerability

- Developing/emerging countries may have to rely more on international disaster relief.
- Developing/emerging countries may not be able to afford expensive coastal defences such as high sea walls to protect against storm surges.
- Developed countries such as the USA can invest in satellite and radar technology to monitor tropical cyclones. The National Hurricane Centre (NHC) in the USA tracks all storms that may have an impact on the Americas, allowing them to alert people and give them time to prepare. Developing/emerging countries cannot afford this complex technology.
- Developing/emerging countries may find it more difficult to rebuild their economies after a tropical cyclone if governments cannot afford to rebuild damaged infrastructure such as roads, railways, ports and airports.

⑤ Exam-style practice   Grades 5–7

Explain **one** reason why Bangladesh is vulnerable to tropical cyclones.

   [3 marks]

Preparing and responding

Tropical cyclones can have significant effects on people and the environment. Countries use different strategies to prepare for tropical cyclones and respond to their impact.

(10) Reducing the hazard risk

Monitoring and prediction

Scientists use weather forecasting and **satellite** and **radar** technology, along with weather charts and complex computer software (including GIS) to track the development and approach of a tropical cyclone. Developing countries are often less prepared, because they cannot afford expensive monitoring technology.

Preparation, warning and evacuation strategies

- Organisations such as the **Red Cross** advise people how to prepare for and respond to a tropical cyclone and its aftermath.
- Countries such as Bangladesh have installed early warning systems that have helped to reduce the death toll.
- People in areas at risk of tropical cyclones are warned when they need to stock up on food and water, as they may be unable to safely leave their houses for days at a time.
- People may be advised to be aware of local evacuation routes and to have a bag of supplies and their essential documents ready, in case they need to evacuate.

Storm surge defences

Strong onshore winds during a tropical cyclone combine with the tide to form storm surges. They can create huge rises in sea level, which can cause extensive coastal flooding. They are one of the most dangerous parts of a tropical cyclone.

High sea walls can be built in coastal areas to help protect against storm surges. Other storm surge defences include barriers that can be raised before a storm to hold back the water.

(5) Named example

- The USA, a developed country, has a sophisticated and effective hurricane monitoring and prediction system. The National Hurricane Center (NHC) in Florida tracks all tropical storm activity in the Atlantic and Eastern Pacific basins because of their potential impact on the Americas.
- When hurricane strength winds are recorded, the NHC, along with the National Weather Service's Weather Forecast Offices, issues a hurricane watch for specific coastal regions to alert people and give them time to prepare.
- The NHC's website also has live updates of expected storm activity, which can be accessed by anyone with an internet connection. This is an effective way of communicating information and giving people time to prepare for a storm.

(5) The Saffir–Simpson scale

The Saffir–Simpson scale classifies tropical cyclones based on their sustained wind speed and their potential for destruction. It has five categories from 1 to 5.

Category	Sustained wind speed in km/h	Damage
1	119–153	• There is some damage to buildings. • Large branches snap. • Damage to power lines cause some power cuts.
2	154–177	• There is major damage to roofs and doors of buildings. • Many shallowly-rooted trees are uprooted. • There are widespread power cuts.
3	178–208	• There is structural damage to buildings. • Numerous roads are blocked by fallen trees. • Electricity and water may be unavailable for several weeks.
4	209–251	• Entire roofs or walls of houses may be destroyed. • Most trees are uprooted. • The area may become uninhabitable for weeks after.
5	252 or above	• Some small buildings will be blown away. • Power cuts may last months. • The area may become uninhabitable for months.

(5) Worked example — Grade 4

A tropical cyclone had sustained wind speeds of 160 km/h and caused major damage to many buildings. State which category this was on the Saffir–Simpson scale. **[1 mark]**

Category 2

(2) Exam-style practice — Grade 4

① Explain **one** way countries can prepare for tropical cyclones. **[2 marks]**

② Explain **one** way satellite images, like **Figure 1** on page 7, are useful in helping to prepare for tropical cyclones. **[2 marks]**

Made a start   Feeling confident   Exam ready

Examples of tropical cyclones

You need to know located examples of how effective methods of preparation and response have been in one developed country and in one emerging or developing country. This page analyses Hurricane Sandy and Typhoon Haiyan.

 Named example

Hurricane Sandy and Typhoon Haiyan

In the USA in 2012, the impacts of Hurricane Sandy included 72 deaths and $71 billion of damage to the economy. In the Philippines in 2013, Typhoon Haiyan was one of the strongest tropical cyclones ever recorded, with 7 m high storm surges. Over 6000 people died and 1.9 million people were left homeless in the Philippines, which is a developing country.

	Hurricane Sandy (developed country)	Typhoon Haiyan (developing country)
Preparations	• The National Hurricane Center (NHC) in Miami predicted and monitored the path of Hurricane Sandy. • Three days before Sandy hit the USA, a state of emergency was declared in areas at risk, including New York. This gave extra powers to government, including the right to evacuate people from their homes. The police evacuated hundreds of thousands of people from coastal areas.	• The Philippine weather agency issued warnings of storm surges two days before Haiyan reached the Philippines. However, many people did not know what the term meant and stayed in their homes. • The government evacuated approximately 750 000 residents. However, many evacuation centres were in areas that were also at risk of flooding from storm surges.
Responses	• 11 000 National Guard troops helped to rescue survivors and keep people safe. • The government provided 16 million litres of water, 14 million meals and 1.5 million blankets. • 8.5 million people lost gas supplies and electricity during the storm. Ten days after the storm, 600 000 people still had no power.	• Immediate responses were slow because of damage to roads. People ran out of water and bodies were not recovered from the streets, increasing the risk of disease. • Military aircraft from the USA, Japan and Singapore arrived within days to help deliver aid relief to remote areas. Approximately $600 million was provided by foreign countries. • 1 million houses were destroyed. The Philippine government was criticised for not providing replacement homes quickly enough. Hundreds of thousands of people continued to live in tents.
Effectiveness	Sandy was the second-largest hurricane ever to hit the USA (after Katrina), but a relatively small number of people died. The preparations and responses were very well planned. The people most at risk were successfully evacuated, and the government provided $2 billion to help people and businesses recover.	The Philippines has an average of 20 tropical cyclones every year, so Filipinos are experienced in dealing with them. However, Haiyan was exceptionally strong. As a result, the preparations and responses were not enough to cope.

 Worked example Grades 5–7

Suggest **two** reasons why tropical cyclones in developing countries often result in a high number of deaths.

[4 marks]

Developing countries do not always have good communication networks, which means that information about a dangerous tropical cyclone approaching might not reach people in vulnerable areas.
Secondly, governments in developing countries may not have the funds to train emergency responders, which means it takes time to rescue people after a tropical cyclone has hit, increasing the death toll.

 Exam-style practice Grades 5–9

'Developing countries cannot prepare effectively for tropical cyclone hazards.' Assess this statement. **[8 marks]**

 Made a start **Feeling confident** **Exam ready**

Earth's layered structure

The Earth's layered structure helps to explain plate motion, which causes tectonic hazards (volcanoes and earthquakes).

⑤ The Earth's layers

- The **inner core** is the hottest part of the Earth, with temperatures of up to 6000 °C. It is mostly made of iron and nickel and it is under so much pressure that it is solid.
- The **outer core** is around the same temperature as the inner core. It is also mostly iron and nickel. However, the outer core is liquid.
- The **mantle** is the thickest layer, with a thickness of around 2900 km. Its temperature is 3700 °C at its boundary with the core and 1000 °C at its boundary with the crust. The upper section of the mantle is called the **asthenosphere**. The asthenosphere is made of magma (semi-molten rock).
- The **crust** is the outer layer of the Earth. At its thickest point, it is only 60 km thick. It is made of solid rock. The temperature of the crust ranges from 200–400 °C.

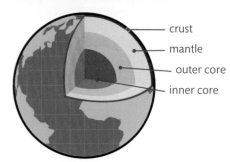

Figure 1 The Earth consists of four main layers.

② Convection

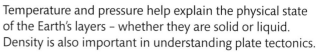
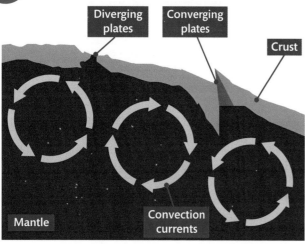

Figure 2 Convection currents in the Earth's mantle cause tectonic plate movement.

The mantle is heated up by the **radioactive decay** of elements in the Earth's core. This process creates **convection currents** in the mantle. This is what drives the movement of tectonic plates in the Earth's crust.

1 Currents of heat energy move up through the mantle from the core.

2 When the currents get near the solid rock of the crust, they stop moving upwards and instead move parallel to the crust/asthenosphere boundary.

3 This movement pulls the tectonic plates in the crust along with it. Convection currents and the movement of the plates are called plate tectonics. The currents then circle back down towards the core.

> There are different theories about the cause of plate movement. Convection is the one you need to know about for your exam.

⑤ Density

Temperature and pressure help explain the physical state of the Earth's layers – whether they are solid or liquid. Density is also important in understanding plate tectonics.

- There are two types of crust: continental crust and oceanic crust.
- Continental crust is less dense than oceanic crust. This is because continental crust is mostly granite, while oceanic crust is mostly basalt, a denser type of rock.
- The asthenosphere is denser than both types of crust. The crust floats on top of it.
- When oceanic crust meets continental crust, it is subducted (pushed underneath) the continental crust because oceanic crust is denser.

② Worked example — Grade 4

The distance from the surface of the crust to the centre of the Earth is around 6371 km.

- The outer core is estimated to be 2200 km thick.
- The mantle is estimated to be 2900 km thick.
- The crust is, on average, 40 km thick.

Based on these figures, calculate the estimated thickness of the inner core. **[1 mark]**

2200 + 2900 + 40 = 5140
6371 − 5140 = 1231 km

⑤ Exam-style practice — Grades 5–7

Explain how convection moves the Earth's tectonic plates. **[3 marks]**

Plate boundary types

There are three main types of plate boundary: divergent, convergent and conservative.

⑮ Plate boundaries

Figure 1 A divergent plate boundary

Figure 2 A convergent plate boundary

Figure 3 A conservative plate boundary

Divergent plate boundaries

- Two plates move away from each other.
- Magma rises to the surface, forming volcanoes. As the magma cools and solidifies, new land and volcanic islands are formed.
- Earthquakes sometimes occur on divergent plate boundaries.

Convergent plate boundaries

- A denser oceanic plate is forced under a less dense continental plate, where it melts and forms magma. Magma is released in violent volcanic eruptions.
- When friction between plates is suddenly released, there are powerful earthquakes.
- The process in which the oceanic plate is pushed under a continental plate is called subduction.

Conservative plate boundaries

- Two plates slide past each other.
- A build-up of friction between the two plates can lead to the sudden release of pressure, causing earthquakes.
- There are no volcanoes at this type of plate boundary. This is because neither new crust is being created nor old crust is being melted.

Figure 4 shows that a few volcanoes also occur far away from plate boundaries. These are usually caused by **hotspots**, fixed places in the mantle where magma rises to the surface in plumes. Magma erupts through the crust as a plate moves over the hotspot. Hotspots in the ocean often create a chain of volcanic islands.

⑤ Worked example Grade 5

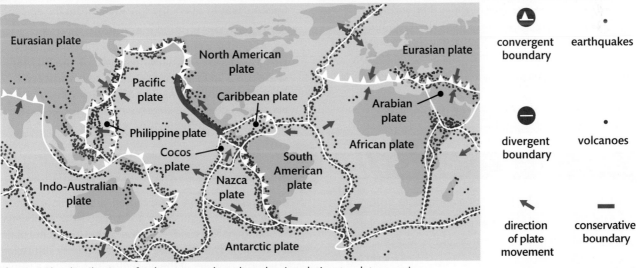

Figure 4 The distribution of volcanoes and earthquakes in relation to plate margins

Study **Figure 4**. Describe the distribution of earthquakes. **[2 marks]**

Figure 4 shows that most earthquakes occur along plate boundaries, and at all three types of plate boundary. A few earthquakes also occur away from plate boundaries, for example in the middle of the Eurasian plate.

② Exam-style practice Grades 5

Suggest **one** reason why conservative plate boundaries do not produce volcanoes. **[2 marks]**

Tectonic hazards

Different factors affect the severity of volcano and earthquake hazards.

 Shield and composite volcanoes

There are two main types of volcano: shield volcanoes and composite volcanoes.

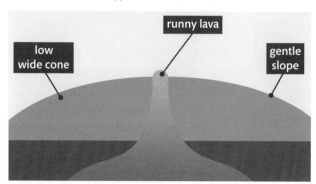

Figure 1 A shield volcano

- **Shield volcanoes** are found on divergent plate boundaries. They have gentle sides.
- Shield volcanoes are formed by eruptions of thin, basaltic magma, which is low in silica and gas. This magma has low viscosity: it is runny and thin.
- Shield volcanoes erupt more frequently than composite volcanoes, but less violently.
- The main hazard is fast-flowing lava, because the lava has low viscosity.

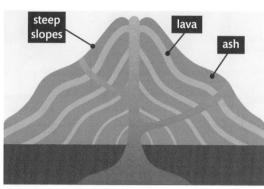

Figure 2 A composite volcano

- **Composite volcanoes** are found on convergent plate boundaries. They have steep sides.
- Composite volcanoes are formed by eruptions of thick magma containing lots of silica and dissolved gas. They produce viscous, acidic lava.
- Composite volcanoes erupt less frequently than shield volcanoes, but more violently.
- Eruptions produce a lot of ash, lava bombs and pyroclastic flows.

 Earthquakes

- Earthquakes are caused when plates are trying to move but get stuck. Pressure builds, and is then suddenly released, releasing large amounts of energy in the Earth's crust. The point where this energy is released and where the earthquake originates is called the **focus**.
- Earthquakes are usually most severe when the focus is near the surface.
- The **epicentre** is the point on the surface that is directly above the earthquake's focus.

- Earthquakes are usually most severe at the epicentre. **Seismic waves** of energy spread out from the epicentre.
- Earthquake size is called **magnitude**. This is a measure of the energy released by the earthquake. Earthquakes are normally measured on the **Richter scale** using an instrument called a **seismometer**. Earthquakes measuring 7 or above are infrequent and very destructive. The largest earthquake ever recorded measured 9.5 on the Richter scale.

 Worked example  Grades 5–7

Study **Figure 2**, which shows a composite volcano. Explain why eruptions from this volcano may be more violent than those from shield volcanoes.

[4 marks]

Composite volcanoes have thick, sticky magma containing a lot of silica. This clogs up the volcano's vent, so pressure builds up inside the volcano, making eruptions very violent. In contrast, shield volcanoes have thin, runny lava that flows smoothly from vents. There is also a lot of dissolved gas trapped in the magma that forms composite volcanoes, which makes their eruptions explosive. In shield volcanoes, there is little gas in the magma.

 Tsunamis

A tsunami is a very large wave caused by tectonic activity. They are most often caused by an earthquake at a convergent plate boundary. The sudden release of pressure as the plates shift causes the crust to move upwards suddenly, displacing a large volume of water at the epicentre. This creates a tsunami. Tsunamis can travel very long distances, but they slow down and increase in height when they reach shallow water. Volcanic eruptions can also cause landslides into or under the ocean, displacing water and causing tsunamis.

 Exam-style practice Grades 5–7

Explain how tectonic activity can cause a tsunami.

[3 marks]

Impacts of earthquakes

Revise your examples of the primary and secondary impacts of earthquakes **or** volcanoes in a developed country and in an emerging or developing country. Only revise this page if you studied earthquakes, not volcanoes.

(2) Primary impacts

Primary impacts are things that happen immediately as a direct result of an earthquake shaking the ground. They include:

- injuries and deaths
- damage to transport and communication links, such as roads that have buckled or bridges that have been destroyed
- damage to and destruction of buildings.

(2) Secondary impacts

Secondary impacts are after-effects that occur in the hours, days and weeks after the earthquake, including:

- the spread of disease because sewage systems are damaged and water becomes polluted
- fires, often because of leaking gas from broken pipelines
- tsunamis, which are secondary impacts because the damage they do is not directly caused by the earthquake shaking the land.

This is a good answer because it gives reasons to explain the primary impacts, it uses primary impacts not secondary ones and it uses specific and relevant case study information to develop the explanations.

(5) Worked example — Grade 7

For a named example you have studied, explain the primary impacts of a recent earthquake. **[4 marks]**

More than 300 000 people were killed in the Haiti earthquake of 2010, mostly because of collapsing buildings. The buildings were not very well constructed and they collapsed when the earthquake, which measured 7.0 on the Richter scale, shook the ground. Another reason why so many people died was that the earthquake hit the densely populated capital of Haiti, Port-au-Prince, which meant that there were many more people impacted than if the earthquake had hit a rural area or smaller town. Another primary impact was that roads were blocked by rubble and other communication links were also damaged or destroyed. Haiti's seaport became unusable because the quays collapsed and the cranes used to unload freight fell into the water.

(5) Factors that increase severity

- Population density affects earthquake severity: earthquakes in uninhabited areas have no human impacts, while earthquakes in densely populated areas can have very severe impacts.
- The stronger the earthquake (the greater its magnitude), the greater the potential for severe primary and secondary impacts.
- Impacts are usually most severe at or near the epicentre of the earthquake.
- Level of development affects both primary and secondary impacts. Developed areas can afford earthquake-proof buildings, while poorly built buildings in poorer areas may collapse. Developing countries may not have sufficient healthcare facilities or emergency services to deal with secondary impacts such as disease or fires.

(10) Exam-style practice — Grades 5–9

Study **Figure 1**, which shows the number of deaths resulting from selected tsunami events.

Year	Location	Number of deaths
1755	Portugal	50 000
1883	Indonesia	34 417
1923	Kamchatka, Russia	2
1945	Pakistan	4000
1946	Alaska, USA	5
2004	Indonesia	175 827
2005	Indonesia	0
2011	Japan	18 451

Figure 1

A student decides to present the data in **Figure 1** as a bar chart. Suggest **one** problem with using this approach. **[2 marks]**

Impacts of volcanoes

Revise your examples of the primary and secondary impacts of earthquakes **or** volcanoes in a developed country and in an emerging or developing country. Only revise this page if you studied volcanoes, not earthquakes.

Primary impacts

Primary impacts are things that happen immediately as a direct result of a volcano erupting. They include:

- people killed or injured, for example by pyroclastic flows, lava flows or volcanic gases
- damage to transport and communication links, for example roads blocked by lava flows
- destruction of buildings
- damage to farmland.

Secondary impacts

Secondary impacts are after-effects of volcanoes that occur in the hours, days and weeks after the eruption. They include:

- pollution of the atmosphere because of ash, which can lead to flights being cancelled
- mudflows (lahars) as rain mixes with ash
- landslides of volcanic debris
- flooding, if lava flows block rivers
- earthquakes triggered by the eruption
- economic impacts, such as a reduction in the number of tourists caused by fear of another eruption.

Factors affecting severity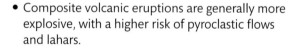

- Composite volcanic eruptions are generally more explosive, with a higher risk of pyroclastic flows and lahars.
- Volcanic eruptions in densely populated regions have more severe impacts.
- The area affected by volcanic ash depends on wind direction and how far up into the atmosphere volcanic ash is carried.
- If a country uses instruments such as tiltmeters and thermal imaging equipment to monitor the volcano, they are more likely to be able to warn people in time for them to evacuate.
- A country's level of development affects the severity of impact. Richer countries can afford extensive volcano monitoring and warning systems so that people can evacuate, while developing countries may not be able to afford them. Secondary impacts are likely to be worse in poorer countries, as they may not have the money to rehouse people or rebuild infrastructure.

Worked example — Grade 7

For a named example you have studied, explain the secondary impacts of a recent volcanic eruption. **[3 marks]**

The Eyjafjallajökull volcano erupted in 2010 and produced an enormous ash cloud that spread eastwards over Europe. About 100 000 flights were cancelled because of the damage the ash did to aeroplane engines. It is estimated that these cancellations cost £80 million.

Another secondary impact was that the glacier covering Eyjafjallajökull melted underneath, which released a large amount of floodwater. Because the volcano has quite steep sides, the water moved very fast and washed away part of a main road, which had to be closed.

In the first paragraph, one point has been made with two connected points and reasons. The connective word 'because' and the facts and figures develop the answer. The first paragraph is sufficient to achieve the full three marks.

Exam focus

If you are given a resource such as a photo, use it to help you consider possible options for your answer. No homes are lava-proof anywhere in the world, which suggests your answer should focus on evacuating people in time.

Exam-style practice — Grade 4

Figure 1 A house catching fire from a lava flow in Hawaii, USA. Hawaii is a chain of volcanic islands caused by a hotspot.

Study **Figure 1**, which shows a house in the path of a lava flow in Hawaii, USA.

Explain **one** reason why the impacts of a volcanic eruption might be less severe in a developed country than in a developing country. **[2 marks]**

 Made a start **Feeling confident** **Exam ready**

Managing earthquake hazards

Revise your examples of how volcanic **or** earthquake hazards are managed in a developed and an emerging or developing country. Only revise this page if you studied earthquakes, not volcanoes.

Planning and preparation

Earthquakes cannot be predicted, but most earthquakes occur in areas with a history of earthquake hazards, so it is possible to prepare for them. Preparation includes:

- earthquake drills (practices), so people know how to respond to an earthquake event.
- specialist training for emergency services, by having regular drills and practice in using specialist lifting equipment.
- tsunami warning systems and earthquake early warning systems
- earthquake-proof buildings
- coastal defences and planning zones for tsunamis.

Exam focus

For longer questions like this, use details and statistics from your located example to strengthen your answer.

Short-term relief

Immediately after an earthquake, people need healthcare, shelter and supplies such as clean water, clothing and food.

In developed countries, specialist rescue teams help emergency services to find people trapped in collapsed buildings. Immediately after the 2011 earthquake and tsunami in Japan, the Japanese government sent specialist rescue teams and 100 000 troops to look for survivors.

In developing and emerging countries, short-term relief is often provided by international aid. This takes time to arrive. No short-term relief was provided by the government in the days after the Haiti earthquake of 2010. Food, water, medical supplies and temporary shelters were flown in from the USA and the Dominican Republic.

Short-term relief for tectonic hazards includes shelter and supplies, while long-term planning includes training and funding emergency services.

 Worked example 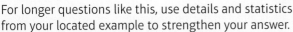 Grade 7

Assess the reasons why earthquake preparation is usually more effective in developed countries than in developing countries. **[8 marks]**

Earthquake preparation involves making buildings earthquake-proof and setting up earthquake warning systems and defences. It is expensive to make buildings earthquake-proof, and developing countries often cannot afford to do this for homes and offices in the way that developed countries can.

In developing countries and emerging countries at risk from earthquakes, builders are usually required by law to use earthquake-proof designs and materials, such as shear walls, cross braces, diaphragms and moment-resisting frames. These help to keep buildings intact in the event of an earthquake and, as a result, save lives. These measures can be expensive and unaffordable for many public and private buildings in developing countries, like Haiti. While the governments in developed countries carry out inspections to make sure buildings are made earthquake-proof in line with the law, in developing and emerging countries it may not always be possible for inspections to take place. As a result, important buildings such as schools and hospitals may collapse when there is an earthquake because they were not built properly.

Earthquake warning systems are another type of preparation. For example, tsunami warnings, which record earthquakes at sea, monitor tsunami waves and transmit evacuation warnings to people living in areas at risk. About 230000 people died from the Indian Ocean tsunami in 2004, mostly in developing and emerging countries. Most of these people did not know that a tsunami was on its way because there was no tsunami warning system for the Indian Ocean and no way of sending warning information to the people living in the coastal zones. Developed countries have the money, governmental organisation and communication networks to make earthquake preparation as effective as possible, but this is less often the case for developing and emerging countries.

Exam-style practice Grade 4

Japan's National Disaster Prevention Day involves practising responses to an earthquake event.

Which of the following describes National Disaster Prevention Day? **[1 mark]**

- [ ] **A** Short-term planning
- [ ] **B** Long-term planning
- [ ] **C** Primary impacts
- [ ] **D** Secondary impacts

Managing volcano hazards

Revise your examples of how volcanic **or** earthquake hazards are managed in a developed and an emerging or developing country. Only revise this page if you studied volcanoes, not earthquakes.

5 Predicting eruptions

Volcanoes can be monitored for the changes that indicate that an eruption is likely. This gives governments enough time to evacuate people.

- Thermal imaging equipment detects increasing temperatures as magma rises to the surface.
- Chemical sensors monitor changes to sulphur gas levels.
- Seismometers measure ground movements, which can be a result of magma rising inside the volcano.
- GPS, tiltmeters and laser beams can measure ground deformation: volcanoes tend to swell before an eruption.

5 Worked example — Grade 7

Study **Figure 1**, which shows computer monitoring of Vesuvius, a volcano near the city of Naples in Italy.

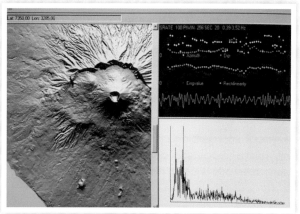

Figure 1 A volcanic monitoring system

Explain how volcanic eruptions can be predicted.

[4 marks]

Volcanic eruptions can be predicted by monitoring changes to volcanoes. Seismometers monitor ground movements. Volcanoes erupt when magma rises up through the rock to the surface. The pressure of the magma cracks underground rocks, and the seismometer records this movement. As the magma builds up under the volcano, the volcano can start to swell. GPS and radar satellites measure this movement and use the data to predict the timing of the eruption, its location on the volcano, and how big it might be.

5 Short-term relief

Immediately after a volcanic eruption, people need healthcare, shelter and supplies such as clean water, clothing and food.

In developed countries, government officials organise short-term relief. This is usually for people who have been evacuated from the areas at risk.

In developing and emerging countries, short-term relief is often provided by international aid. This takes time to arrive.

Because it is possible to monitor volcanoes effectively, short-term relief usually involves caring for evacuated people. Developed countries have the money needed to research, develop, install and maintain the best volcano monitoring.

5 Planning, preparation and prediction

Hazard maps use volcano monitoring data and records of the areas affected during past eruptions, in order to show which areas are likely to be affected by different types of volcanic hazard. They are used to plan evacuations and to make sure hospitals, evacuation centres and other key institutions are not in high-risk areas.

Planning and practising evacuations enable people to escape quickly and safely. Exclusion zones may also be set up in high-risk areas. People are not allowed to live in these zones and access to them is limited.

Short-term relief includes shelter and supplies. Long-term planning includes training and funding emergency services.

Exam focus

For a 4 mark **explain** question, you should develop two relevant points, supported by examples or details to show your understanding.

This is a very similar question to the worked example for earthquakes on page 15. Study the worked example answer and use it as a model for answering this question.

2 Exam-style practice — Grades 5–9

Assess the reasons why volcanic eruption prediction is usually more effective in developed countries than in developing countries.

[8 marks]

Development

Countries are usually described as 'developed' if they have a high income, a good quality of life or a high level of equality. There are contrasting ways of defining development.

 ## Economic measures – advantages and disadvantages

One economic measure of development is **Gross Domestic Product (GDP) per capita**. GDP per capita is the value of all the goods and services produced within a country, divided by the number of people in the population. This is called a single index because it measures one thing: value.

👍 GDP per capita is a straightforward way to measure the wealth of a country.

👍 GDP per capita makes it easy to compare one country with another.

👎 GDP per capita does not measure quality of life.

👎 GDP per capita does not show inequality. A country with a high GDP per capita may have some very rich people and a large proportion of the population living in poverty.

 ## Social measures of development

Social measures of development show whether people in a country can expect to live a long and healthy life. Social measures of development include life expectancy, infant mortality rate and literacy rate.

The **Human Development Index (HDI)** is a **composite index** of development because it combines three measures, including social and economic measures: Gross National Income (GNI) per capita, life expectancy and number of years in education. This generates an average score from 0 to 1, with 1 being the highest.

👍 HDI can reveal development differences between countries with the same GDP.

👍 HDI is produced by the United Nations so the data is reliable and covers most countries.

👎 Like GDP, HDI can hide inequalities between regions within a country.

👎 Quality of life depends on lots of different factors, not just education and life expectancy.

 ## Measures of inequality

There is inequality between countries, in that developed countries have high incomes and developing countries have lower incomes. There is also inequality within countries.

- Inequality within a country is measured using the **Gini coefficient** – a coefficient between 0 and 1. The closer a country's score is to 0, the more equal it is. The closer it is to 1, the more inequality there is.

- Corruption can be a problem in developing countries and countries where there is a lack of democracy (i.e. where citizens don't get a vote on who governs the country). Political corruption is when government officials use their power and public money to make money for themselves, rather than using it on aid or services, such as health and education, to benefit the people of the country.

- The Corruption Perceptions Index grades countries from 'highly corrupt' (0) to 'very clean' (100).

- In 2017, Denmark had a Corruption Perceptions Index of 88 while Venezuela was 18. For Gini, Denmark was ranked at 32.6 while Venezuela was 44.8.

Geographical skills

Describe the distribution of the colours and patterns on the map, and how they relate to particular countries or parts of the world.

 ## Worked example — Grades 5–7

no data

very high HDI score   very low HDI score

Figure 1 Map showing countries by their HDI score

Study **Figure 1**, a map showing HDI score.

Compare the differences in HDI score between Africa and North America. **[3 marks]**

HDI combines three levels of development, including GNI per capita, so North America's very high HDI scores reflect the high level of GNI per capita in the USA and Canada. In contrast, while Africa has some countries that have relatively high HDI scores, no African countries are as developed as the USA and Canada. A second difference is that while the countries of North America have the same HDI levels, the countries of Africa have a wide range of different levels of HDI, from relatively high in north Africa to very low in central Africa.

 ## Exam-style practice — Grades 4–5

Describe how **one** social measure is used to define development. **[2 marks]**

Levels of development

Countries at different levels of development have differences in their demographic data.

⑤ Key terms

- **Demographic data** – data about a population
- **Fertility rate** – average births per woman
- **Death rate** – deaths per 1000 people per year
- **Population structure** – number of males and females per age group in a population
- **Maternal mortality rate** – number of women who die in childbirth for every 100 000 women who give birth
- **Infant mortality rate** – number of babies who die in their first year per 1000 live births

⑤ Demographic data and development

Development causes demographic data to change.

- Modern medicine can cause life expectancies to increase, so the **death rate** decreases as a country develops.
- Development reduces the **infant mortality rate**. As a country develops, more children survive.
- Development reduces **fertility rates**, as educated women with careers tend to delay having children. Contraception also reduces fertility rates. Couples may have smaller families to help them enjoy a higher standard of living. On the other hand, many people in developing countries have large families so that more people are available to work.

⑩ Population pyramids

Population pyramids show the population structure of a country. The impact of development on population structure can be seen by comparing population pyramids for developing, emerging and developed countries.

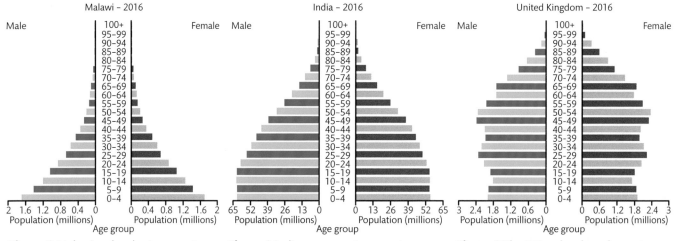

Figure 1 Malawi, a developing country

Most of the population of Malawi is under 30. Infant mortality rates have dropped, but fertility rates are still high.

Figure 2 India, an emerging country

Many more people are surviving into middle age in India as the death rate drops. The middle of the graph is much wider than the top.

Figure 3 The UK, a developed country

In the UK, the birth rate is declining as couples decide to have fewer children and have children later. There is an ageing population, with many more people surviving into old age than in the past.

⑤ Worked example — Grades 4–5

In Malawi, the fertility rate in 2017 was 5.49 children per woman. In the UK it was 1.88. Suggest **one** reason for this difference. **[3 marks]**

In Malawi, women may not have access to education or be able to get jobs. Instead, they marry young and have large families. In the UK, all women have the opportunity to get a good education and access to jobs. Many decide to have children later and have fewer children so they can work and progress in their careers.

② Exam-style practice — Grade 4

Using **Figures 1**, **2 and 3**, explain why India is an emerging country. **[4 marks]**

Made a start   Feeling confident   Exam ready

Global inequalities

Wealth is not evenly distributed across the world. Here are some reasons for global inequality.

(10) Causes of global inequalities

There are environmental, historical, social, economic and political reasons for global inequalities.

Climate (environmental)
Extreme weather hazards, such as tropical cyclones, may inhibit a country's ability to develop due to the frequent devastation they can cause. Countries with a tropical climate may be inhibited by people regularly suffering from tropical diseases.

Healthcare and education (social)
Countries that have invested in education and healthcare are generally more developed.

International relations (economic and political)
Countries that have opened up to global trade have grown faster than countries that have put up barriers to globalisation.

Causes of global inequalities

Colonialism (historical)
Colonialism means acquiring political control over another country and economically exploiting it. Colonialism has led to the uneven development of some richer nations in comparison to the countries that they colonised.

Neo-colonialism (historical)
Rich countries today still use their power to dominate poorer countries.

Topography (environmental)
Countries with hostile landscapes, such as desert or mountains, may find it harder to develop, as it can be difficult to build transport infrastructure or produce enough food.

Systems of governance (political)
Countries with corrupt or unstable governments develop more slowly, as investment in infrastructure, healthcare and education is inadequate.

(5) Income quintiles

One way to show the scale of inequality between countries is to use **income quintiles**. These are calculated by the World Bank.

1. All 230 countries are put in order by GDP per capita. Currently the USA is at the top.

2. The list is divided into five equal groups of 46 countries. Each group is called a quintile.

3. The top quintile, containing the 46 richest countries in the world, currently owns more than 80 per cent of all GDP. This means the top 20 per cent of countries own 80 per cent of all wealth.

4. The bottom two quintiles (bottom 40 per cent of countries) own just 3 per cent of all GDP.

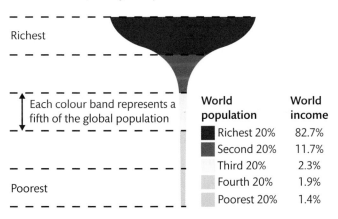

Richest

Each colour band represents a fifth of the global population

Poorest

	World population	World income
Richest 20%		82.7%
Second 20%		11.7%
Third 20%		2.3%
Fourth 20%		1.9%
Poorest 20%		1.4%

Figure 2 Income quintiles show income inequality globally.

(2) Consequences

Global inequality causes people to migrate in search of a safer, healthier and more prosperous life. There are economic, social and political reasons for international migration.

Economic: More than 3 billion people live on less than $2.50 per day. This affects living standards and quality of life. People migrate to countries with better pay and more opportunities.

Social: 1 in 9 people in the world do not have clean water where they live. Without clean water or access to healthcare, millions of people do not reach their full potential.

Political: Many people in developing countries want to live in safer countries with less corruption.

(5) Worked example   Grades 5–7

Explain **one** way in which environmental factors contribute to global inequalities.   **[2 marks]**

Climate change has environmental impacts that contribute to inequalities between countries, because some developing countries are much more vulnerable to impacts, such as sea level rise or drought, than the most developed countries. While a country like the USA will be able to afford higher sea defences to protect key infrastructure from sea level rise, some developing countries cannot afford this and sea level rise will damage coastal roads, railways, power plants and homes. This will make it harder for these countries to develop, increasing global inequalities.

(2) Exam-style practice   Grades 4–5

Explain why international migration is a consequence of inequality between countries.   **[4 marks]**

✓ **Made a start**   ✓ **Feeling confident**   ✓ **Exam ready**

Theories of development

You need to know about two theories of how and why countries develop over time: Rostow's modernisation theory and Frank's dependency theory.

⑤ Rostow's modernisation theory ✓

Rostow believed that countries passed through five stages of development.

❶ In a traditional society, most people farm to grow the food that they eat.

❷ Manufacturing grows, farmers grow crops to sell at markets and trading increases.

❸ Industries grow rapidly, communication links improve and overseas trade produces significant profit, which powers more growth.

❹ Steady growth continues, technology develops, making processes more efficient, and new industries replace outdated ones.

❺ Growth comes from people in the country buying more and more products, creating more demand for more industries.

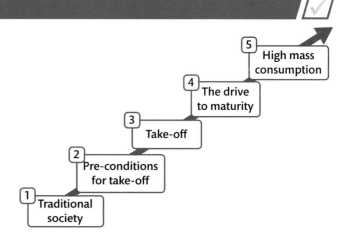

Figure 1 The five stages of Rostow's modernisation theory

Rostow believed capitalism powered development. But capitalism also creates inequalities.

Rostow developed his theory from studying how European countries had developed. However, the development of some countries shows that not all countries have to necessarily follow the same steps.

⑤ Frank's dependency theory ✓

Frank was critical of capitalism.

• Frank believed the most developed countries had usually been colonial powers. They had exploited other countries to make themselves rich.

• According to Frank, the capitalist global trading system was designed to benefit the developed countries. These countries made sure developing countries remained dependent on them for trade.

• In Frank's theory, the economic core (developed countries) exploits the economic periphery (developing countries). The core develops at the expense of the periphery.

Frank's theory does not explain how some countries that used to be colonies have now become developed, such as Singapore, while others have not.

Frank's theory says that the core exploits the periphery. However, global trade has been responsible for helping millions of people to escape poverty in the last twenty years, for example in China.

Frank believed socialism would develop countries more fairly. But most developing countries that have adopted socialism remain poor and unequal.

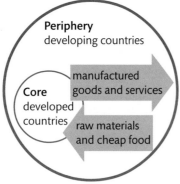

Figure 2 Frank's dependency theory is based on a core of developed countries exploiting developing countries (the periphery).

② Worked example　　Grade 5 ✓

Describe **one** feature of Rostow's modernisation theory of development. **[2 marks]**

In Rostow's theory countries progress through five stages from traditional society, which is undeveloped, to high mass consumption, which is when a country is modernised.

⑩ Exam-style practice　　Grades 7–9 ✓

Explain how Rostow's theory can be used to show how countries develop over time. **[4 marks]**

 Made a start **Feeling confident** **Exam ready**

Approaches to development

Countries can try various approaches to development, including top-down and bottom-up strategies. All development is affected by globalisation. Some countries have benefited more than others from globalisation.

 Top-down and bottom-up strategies

Top-down strategies

- Top-down projects are usually large-scale. This means they aim to develop a whole country or region, for example building dams that provide electricity for thousands of people.
- Decisions are made by governments or large companies, not by local people.
- Top-down schemes are extremely expensive, costing millions or billions of pounds, and are sometimes funded by international development banks.
- The technology involved is often extremely sophisticated and expensive to maintain.

Bottom-up strategies

- Bottom-up projects are local-scale projects that aim to help a community or small area to develop. An example is building a well so that a community has access to safe, clean water.
- Decisions are made by the local people affected by the project.
- Bottom-up projects are usually much cheaper than top-down projects. They may be funded by the local community.
- The technology involved is kept simple so that local people can operate it and repair it.

 Globalisation

Globalisation is the increasing interconnectedness and interdependence of the world, especially economically. A government can promote the globalisation of its country by reducing regulations for foreign businesses. For example, they can allow transnational corporations (TNCs) to pay low taxes.

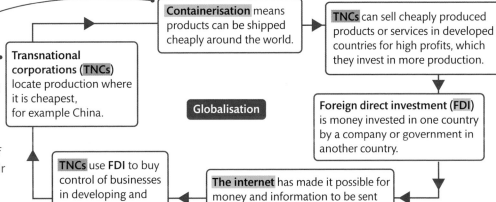

Figure 1 Flow diagram showing the processes and players that contribute to globalisation

 Worked example   Grades 5–7

Explain why TNCs invest in developing countries.
[4 marks]

TNCs invest in developing countries in order to produce products as cheaply as possible. They need a cheap labour force that is educated enough for workers to be trained. The TNC can find these workers in some developing countries. Governments of developing countries want to have the benefits that the TNCs will bring, especially investment and the jobs that they will create. This means that governments will provide tax incentives for the TNCs that wish to invest in their country.

 Exam-style practice   Grade 4

Which of the following is a characteristic of a bottom-up strategy? **[1 mark]**

- [ ] **A** Experts work with locals to identify their needs.
- [ ] **B** It aims to develop a region or nation.
- [ ] **C** Local people have no say in the project.
- [ ] **D** It may have large-scale negative environmental consequences.

Advantages and disadvantages

Different approaches to development have their advantages and disadvantages. You need to know about the advantages and disadvantages of NGO-led intermediate technology, investment by TNCs and IGO-funded large infrastructure.

⑤ Key terms

- ☑ **Non-governmental organisations (NGOs)** are organisations (often charities) who are independent of governments and many have expertise in development issues.
- ☑ **Intergovernmental organisations (IGOs)** are groups of different countries working together. Examples include the United Nations and the World Bank, both of which help to organise development projects.
- ☑ **Intermediate technology** is simple technology that local people can use and repair for themselves.
- ☑ **Transnational corporations (TNCs)** are companies that operate in at least two countries.

⑤ NGO-led intermediate technology

- 👍 Local people have a good understanding of what they need most. Working directly with local communities gives NGO-led development schemes a better chance of meeting local needs and being used and improved.
- 👍 Intermediate technology means local people can be trained to maintain the project and fix it if it breaks.
- 👎 The project only helps a small number of people.
- 👎 Governments in developing countries may rely on NGOs too much, instead of developing their own solutions to people's problems.

② Worked example   Grades 4–5

Study **Figure 1**, which shows a rainwater harvesting project in use in India.

Figure 1 Rainwater is captured in the rainy season and stored for use in the dry season.

Suggest **two** characteristics of the project that make it an example of intermediate technology.   **[2 marks]**

Rainwater capture is a very simple technology which is easy for local people to use. It is small-scale technology that uses local resources (i.e. rainwater) and it is sustainable, as it does not require electricity to make it work.

Exam focus

For a 2-mark **suggest** question like this, you need to make a clear, developed point to get both marks.

⑤ TNC investment

- 👍 Investment by TNCs creates jobs, develops skills and introduces modern technology into developing and emerging countries.
- 👍 Other industries and services often grow up around TNC-funded businesses. This **multiplier effect** boosts development.
- 👎 TNCs may pull their investment out of an area if they find a cheaper location for production.
- 👎 Some TNCs may permit poor working conditions that would not be tolerated in developed countries.

⑤ IGO-funded large infrastructure

- 👍 IGOs can access very large amounts of money, allowing huge projects such as dams to be constructed in developing countries.
- 👍 Very large numbers of people can benefit. For example, whole regions can gain access to electricity or a water supply for irrigating their crops.
- 👎 There can be negative consequences for some people. For example, the reservoirs, created by constructing dams, often flood inhabited land.
- 👎 The huge amounts of money involved in IGO-funded large infrastructure projects can encourage corruption; people may steal the money.

② Exam-style practice   Grade 4

Which of the following would be an example of an IGO-funded large infrastructure development project?
     [1 mark]

- ☐ **A** A network of canals to irrigate 2 million hectares of farmland
- ☐ **B** A village biogas plant, powered by cow dung
- ☐ **C** Toilet facilities for a town district
- ☐ **D** A new factory, funded by TNC investment

Emerging economy: India

You need to know a case study about the development of **one** of the world's emerging countries. It is important that you know where the country you have studied is, and how this has affected its development. This case study is about development in India.

15 Case study

India in the world

India is now the second most populous nation on the planet, with 1.3 billion inhabitants. It is also the seventh largest economy in the world. Since economic reforms in 1991, it has experienced rapid economic development that has enabled it to be grouped with other rapidly-emerging economies, known as the **BRICS** (Brazil, Russia, India, China and South Africa).

- **Site:** refers to the country's location (where it is in the world and which continent and hemisphere it is in). India is a large country located in South East Asia. The Tropic of Cancer runs through the north of India.

- **Situation:** relates to its surroundings, both physical and human. The west coast of India is on the Arabian Sea, while the Bay of Bengal and Indian Ocean can be found off the east coast. The north of India shares international borders with seven other countries including, Bangladesh, Pakistan and China.

- **Connectivity:** refers to how well a country is connected to its neighbours and the wider world. India was once part of the British Empire and still has a close relationship with the UK today.

Society and culture

- In 2018, India had a population of 1.3 billion and was the second most populous country in the world.

- In 2018, life expectancy for women was 70.3 years and for men 67.4 years.

- India has a world-famous history and culture. The Indian film industry, which includes Bollywood, makes more than 1600 films a year, seen by over 2.7 billion people.

Politics

- The country is a member of the World Trade Organization and the UN.

- India is the world's largest democracy and a federal republic, made up of 29 states.

Figure 1 India's site and situation

Environment

- India has a range of contrasting environments – in the north are the foothills of the Himalayan mountains and in the south is the upland Deccan Plateau. The River Ganges flows through the fertile floodplains in the north-east and out into the Bay of Bengal. The Thar Desert is also located in the north-east.

- The country experiences two monsoon seasons: the north-east monsoon and the south-west monsoon. These occur at different times within the overall monsoon season of June to October.

- In 2014, India was ranked 155th out of 178 countries for its environmental quality.

5 Worked example   Grade 5–6

Explain **one** way in which a country's history can affect its economic development.   **[2 marks]**

Some countries, like India, were once governed by other countries. Until 1947, India was part of the British Empire and today continues to be part of the Commonwealth. This means it still has a close trading relationship with the UK. Many UK companies, like BT, have outsourced parts of their business to India.

5 Exam-style practice   Grades 5–6

Explain **one** way that environmental factors can affect a country's economic development.   **[2 marks]**

India: Economic change and development

Emerging countries have undergone rapid economic growth in recent times. For your case study country, you need to understand how and why its economy has grown.

(5) Economy

India's Gross Domestic Product (GDP) is US $2.3 trillion (for comparison, the UK's is US $2.6 trillion). India's Gross National Income (GNI) per capita in 2017 was US $7760. In 1990, it was US $1220.

(2) Regional influence

India has emerged as an important regional power. As a rising economic and nuclear power and with a population of over 1.3 billion, India's increasing affluence has provided a growing market for its neighbours to trade with.

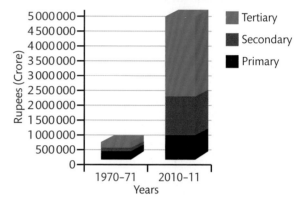

Figure 1 India's GDP by economic sector

(5) Key economic trends

- Manufacturing industries – the secondary sector of the economy – have rapidly expanded in India in recent years. This has been encouraged by government initiatives such as Make in India, which is intended to make India a global manufacturing hub and create millions of jobs.

- The secondary sector's contribution to India's economy has risen, while the contribution of the primary sector, particularly agriculture, has declined. In 1991, 64 per cent of people worked in agriculture while in 2017 it was 43 per cent. This has led to increased migration from rural areas to urban areas. The services sector, or tertiary sector, now makes the biggest contribution to India's GDP (61 per cent). This has resulted in a more skilled workforce and is reducing poverty.

- Parts of India's quaternary sector have grown rapidly, particularly the telecommunications network. Investments from transnational corporations (TNCs) have contributed to this change.

(5) Globalisation

- In the 1990s, the Indian government adopted a pro-foreign direct investment (pro-FDI) policy and opened up its markets to global trade. Foreign companies no longer had to pay high taxes on profits that they made in India. The government reduced controls on how much money could be invested in India from abroad.

- By 2005, many TNCs were investing in India – it was second only to China for the amount of FDI it received.

- One strong area of growth was telecommunications. Because of India's history as part of the British Empire, English is one of many languages spoken in India. Many TNCs outsourced their call centres to India, as wage costs were much lower than in many other countries.

- Some multinational companies, such as Toyota, manufacture cars in India.

- Historically, India has received over £200 million a year from the UK government in aid. In 2015, the UK government significantly reduced aid to India because the economy had grown so much.

(10) Exam-style practice   Grades 5–7

1. For a named emerging country, explain **two** ways in which globalisation has affected that country's development.
   [4 marks]

2. Study **Figure 1**. Describe how the economy has changed since 1970.
   [3 marks]

3. Suggest **one** reason for the changes in India's economy, shown in **Figure 1**.
   [2 marks]

 Made a start **Feeling confident** **Exam ready**

India: Impacts of development

You may need to answer questions about an emerging country that is managing to develop, using a case study you have revised. This case study looks at the impacts of development in India.

Demographic change

Rapid economic change contributes to demographic change.

- In India, the fertility rate has fallen from approximately 5.2 children born per woman in 1971 to 2.3 in 2018.
- The death rate per 1000 people has fallen from 10.59 in 1991 to 7.31 in 2016.

These changes have happened as access to healthcare, education and employment have increased.

Water pollution and air pollution both have serious impacts on human health. Air pollution can cause respiratory problems, while polluted water can carry diseases such as cholera and typhoid.

 Environmental impacts

Rapid development has had a number of negative environmental impacts in India.

- Air pollution is a serious problem: 13 of the world's top 20 polluted cities are in India. Delhi is one of the world's most polluted city. This is mainly due to a rapid increase in the numbers of cars, motorbikes and lorries.
- Water pollution: India's rivers, such as the Ganges, are badly polluted and a major risk to health. This is mainly because of big increases in the amount of untreated human sewage going into rivers.
- Rapid development has led to increased greenhouse gas emissions, which contributes to climate change. India is the world's third largest emitter of carbon dioxide after China and the USA. This is mainly because India relies on coal as its main energy source.

Urbanisation and regional development

Rapid economic change has caused urbanisation.

- In 2018, 33 per cent of the population lived in urban areas; in 1901 only 11 per cent of India's population lived in urban areas.
- Urbanisation is driven by rural–urban migration: people leaving the countryside to find work in cities.
- City growth is driven by the demand for more houses and jobs. India has two of the world's five largest cities: Mumbai and Delhi.

These changes have created regions with different socio-economic characteristics. In 2018, India's richest state, Goa, had a Gross Domestic Product (GDP) per capita approximately 10 times higher than Bihar, India's poorest state. Bihar is a rural state, where most people still work in farming, whereas Goa has a thriving tourist industry.

International influence

As emerging countries become more important to global trade, they have more geopolitical influence in their region and internationally.

- India is becoming less dependent on aid from Europe and the USA. In 2015, the UK government significantly reduced the aid given to India.
- India is a member of the G20. This is an influential group of the world's 20 most developed economies, including the USA and countries in the European Union (EU).
- India's strong economy has led to it becoming stronger militarily. This makes India seem more threatening to its neighbours, especially Pakistan.
- Indian companies are important for foreign direct investment (FDI). India is able to support investment in developing countries. It has also invested in steel making and car making in the UK.

Worked example — Grade 6

For a named emerging country, explain how rapid economic change has contributed to demographic change. **[4 marks]**

As India has become wealthier, life expectancy has increased because housing quality, access to healthcare and access to clean water has improved. The fertility rate has fallen from 5.2 children per woman in 1971 to 2.3 children in 2018.
This decrease is linked to rapid economic change as people, especially women, who work in services are better paid and tend to have fewer children.

Exam-style practice — Grades 5–7

In 2014, Goa had a GDP per capita of $5498.
The mean GDP per capita for India was $1395.

Calculate how many times higher the GDP per capita for Goa was than the mean GDP per capita for India. **[2 marks]**

India and globalisation

You need to know about changes that have happened in your case study country as a result of economic development and globalisation, and different views of these changes. This page looks at India.

(10) Age and gender

👍 Younger people have benefited from new jobs created by foreign direct investment (FDI). This is because younger people are more likely to leave rural areas and move to the cities for the new jobs (rural–urban migration).

👍 Economic development has made more jobs available. India's growing middle classes now have access to a huge range of interesting and well-paid jobs in industry and services.

👍 Women have benefited from better healthcare, which has reduced the maternal mortality rate to 174 per 100 000 births in 2015. The rate was 556 per 100 000 births in 1990.

👎 New jobs created as a result of FDI have not benefited older people. As young people have moved to the cities, older people have been left behind. Older people are often left in charge of grandchildren whose parents are working in the cities. Older people are also often left to work the family farm.

👎 Not all the new jobs offer good pay and conditions. 21 per cent of Indians live on less than $1.90 per day. People who are poor will work long hours for low pay, for example, in India's many textile factories.

👎 India's women are discriminated against for social and cultural reasons, especially in rural areas.

(2) Benefits of TNC investment

India is attractive to TNC investment because of its skilled labour force (e.g. many English-language speakers), low labour costs, growing middle class and government tax breaks for TNCs.

👍 Transnational corporations (TNCs) have created jobs and trained and educated their employees.

👍 TNCs pay tax to the government, which can then be invested in social improvements.

👍 TNCs create a multiplier effect for economic development.

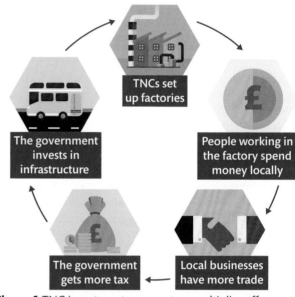

Figure 1 TNC investment can create a multiplier effect.

(2) Worked example · Grade 6

Explain how changing international relations have costs and benefits for a named emerging country.
[4 marks]

India's importance in global trade means it can now make strong demands in trade deals with developed countries. For example, in return for a trade deal with the EU, India can demand rights for Indians to move to the EU to live and work.

A cost of India's growing importance in the world is that there is more international pressure on the country to help solve global warming. This would mean more government controls that Indian people might not accept. For example, controls on vehicle emissions would make transport more expensive, and reductions in the use of coal could make electricity more expensive.

(2) Costs of TNC investment

Not all the impacts of TNC investment have been positive for India. For example:

👎 Some TNCs have created a lot of pollution, taking advantage of the relaxed environmental laws in India.

👎 Many TNCs are owned by foreign countries, so **economic leakage** occurs. This is when profits are sent abroad to the TNC's headquarters.

👎 TNCs often produce products that are cheaper and better marketed than local products. Local producers are outcompeted and close down.

(2) Exam-style practice · Grade 4

Study **Figure 1**, which shows the multiplier effect of TNC investment.

Explain **one** way foreign investment can increase economic development in a developing country.
[2 marks]

Urbanisation trends

Urbanisation is the increase in numbers of people living in urban areas compared to rural areas.

⑤ Urbanisation patterns and trends

In 1980, 39.3 per cent of the world's population lived in urban areas. In 2017, this had increased to 54.8 per cent. By 2050, this percentage will have increased again, with more than 6 billion people living in urban areas. **Urbanisation** is happening faster in developing and emerging countries than in developed countries, because developed countries are already extremely urbanised. Cities in developed countries may also have problems like transport congestion and a lack of affordable housing, which can lead to **counter-urbanisation**.

Between now and 2050, 90 per cent of the expected increase in the world's urban population will take place in Africa and Asia. Between them, India, China and Nigeria are expected to account for 37 per cent of the projected growth of the world's urban population by 2050. In contrast, in 2017, the UK's population was 83 per cent urbanised. By 2050, it is estimated that the UK's population will be 90 per cent urbanised.

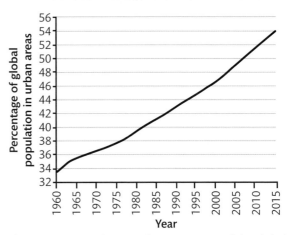

Figure 1 A graph showing the percentage of the global population living in urban areas.

② Urban primacy

Urban primacy occurs when a city grows at the expense of the area around it. The city 'sucks' people and resources out of the surrounding area, because everyone wants to go there to work and no one wants to invest anywhere else. The city becomes the core (see page 54) and the area around the edge of the city is called the hinterland. As the hinterland becomes poorer, even more people move to the city, leading to a downwards spiral.

⑤ Calculating percentage change

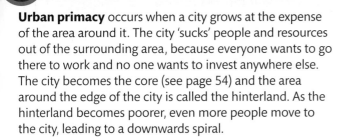

You need to know how to calculate the percentage increase of city growth.

❶ Work out the increase by calculating the difference between the two numbers you are comparing.

new number − original number = increase

❷ Then divide the increase by the original number and multiply by 100.

Use the same process to calculate percentage decrease:

original number − new number = decrease

⑤ Megacities

- A megacity is a city with over 10 million inhabitants.
- Over the last 15–20 years, the number of megacities has increased rapidly.
- Some megacities in developed countries, such as Tokyo in Japan, have a population of over 35 million people.
- The majority of megacities are in Asia, where there are many countries with emerging economies and rapid rates of urbanisation. There are five megacities in India alone.
- Between now and 2050, the majority of new megacities are likely to appear in developing and emerging countries.

Figure 2 The location of the world's 10 largest megacities in 2018. The population of Tokyo was 37.5 million.

① Worked example   Grade 5

Explain **one** reason why urban primacy can become a problem in rapidly urbanising countries. **[2 marks]**

Urban primacy causes the hinterland around the urban area to be deprived of growth, investment and resources.

② Exam-style practice   Grade 5

Mumbai's population in 1991 was 9.9 million. By 2015 Mumbai's population had increased to 13 million. Calculate the percentage increase in Mumbai's population. **[2 marks]**

Growing cities

Economic change and migration are processes that contribute to the growth decline of cities, both within the country and internationally.

 ## Factors affecting urbanisation

Migration

Rural–urban migration is when people move from rural areas to urban areas, usually within the same nation. It increases the rate of urbanisation. This type of migration characterises emerging countries, as they often have many manufacturing jobs in urban areas for which people leave rural areas. Many migrants are young economically active people, who start families resulting in an increase in the birth rate and the overall population.

Counter-urbanisation is when people move from urban to rural areas, usually within the same nation, often in search of a better quality of life. This type of migration characterises developed countries. Reasons for migration can be categorised as either **push factors** or **pull factors**.

- Push factors are reasons that people leave a place, such as a lack of key services, poor transport links and low-paid employment.
- Pull factors are things that attract people to a place, such as good medical facilities, a range of entertainment options and higher-paid employment.

International migration

Cities also grow because of international migration from other countries. The main reason for this is economic: most cities have a wide variety of very well-paid jobs, which attract highly skilled workers from around the world.

Economic change

As more people arrive in a city, this boosts the city's economy, making it even more attractive to migrants. This is called a multiplier effect.

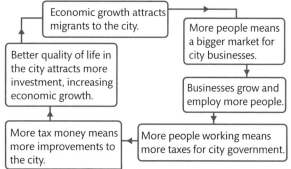

Figure 1 Flow diagram showing a multiplier effect

Worked example — Grades 5–7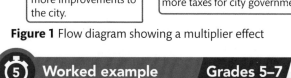

Explain the factors that affect the rate of urbanisation. **[4 marks]**

One of the main factors that affect the rate of urbanisation is rural–urban migration. People living in rural areas will often choose to move to urban areas, influenced by push and pull factors. For example, in the countryside the main source of income is farming, which is low paid. Many people move to the cities in search of higher-paid employment. Another factor affecting the rate of urbanisation is natural increase, which is when the birth rate is higher than the death rate. Natural increase tends to be higher in urban areas.

Declining cities

- If a city's economic growth slows down, the city may start to decline.
- If many city companies start to close down or reduce the numbers of people they employ, people may move away from the city.
- Investment will also move to other locations where there is better economic growth.
- A **downwards spiral** may result from this. The city becomes run-down and crime rates may increase.
- Cities are more likely to decline in developed countries. For example, the city of Detroit in the USA has lost more than half its population since 1950.

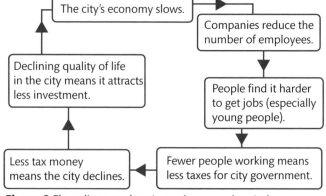

Figure 2 Flow diagram showing a downwards spiral

Exam-style practice — Grades 2–3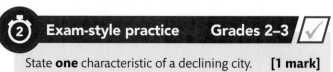

State **one** characteristic of a declining city. **[1 mark]**

 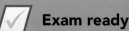

Different urban economies

Urban economies are different in developed, emerging and developing countries. You need to know about differences in types of employment, working conditions and the size of economic sectors.

(10) Formal and informal employment

- Formal employment refers to jobs that involve paying taxes, have a regular wage and offer some legal protection to workers. Most jobs in developed countries are formal.
- Informal employment refers to jobs that the government does not collect tax from because they are unofficial. These jobs are easy for new arrivals to a city in a developing or emerging country to get, but workers are not protected by law.

Formal employment	Informal employment
Workers usually work for an established business, for example, in an office, factory or organisation.	Workers usually work for themselves, often on the street.
Employees have rights protected by law, for example, minimum wage laws and health and safety laws.	Workers do not have rights. If they are ill they do not get paid. There are no minimum wages.
Employees pay tax to the government.	Workers do not pay tax. This is illegal, so they are at risk of arrest.
If employees can join a trade union, they will be able to campaign for higher pay and better conditions.	Workers may need to pay protection money to gangs, or risk being attacked and robbed by the gangs.
Working conditions are usually regulated: companies have to provide a safe place to work.	Working conditions are often unhealthy or dangerous and workers may be expected to work long hours.

(5) Economic sectors

Primary sector

The primary sector is much less important than the secondary and tertiary sectors in both developing and emerging cities. In developed countries, only a tiny proportion of people in urban areas work in the primary sector.

Secondary sector

Urban economies in emerging countries tend to be dominated by the secondary sector, such as manufacturing.

Today, developing countries often have secondary industries that process primary products such as sugar. This means the secondary sector is also significant in urban economies in developing countries. The secondary sector is less important in the urban economies of developed countries.

Many migrants move from rural areas, where they have been involved in agriculture, to urban areas to find better paid employment in new secondary sector industries. These migrants are often young economically active people who start families, resulting in an increase in the birth rate and population (natural increase).

Tertiary sector

The tertiary sector is employment in services. The service sector is important to urban economies in emerging countries because of government jobs, tourism and transport industries. In developing countries, tertiary sector jobs tend to be informal, such as barbers or street traders.

In the urban economies of most developed countries, the tertiary sector is dominant in that it produces the most GDP and employs the most people.

(2) Worked example — Grade 5

Study **Figure 1**, which shows a textile factory in an emerging country.

Figure 1 This type of work can involve long hours and low pay.

Identify which economic sector is shown. **[1 mark]**

☐	**A** Primary sector
☒	**B** Secondary sector
☐	**C** Tertiary sector
☐	**D** Quaternary sector

(5) Exam-style practice — Grades 5–7

Explain **one** reason why working conditions in developing countries and emerging countries may be worse than in developed countries. **[3 marks]**

Changing cities

The size and distribution of the population of cities and land use in different areas of a city change over time.

⑩ Land use

Land use, population distribution and growth in a city change over time. The main factors affecting land use are accessibility, availability, cost and planning regulations.

1. Mostly commercial land use – the CBD is often where the city first developed. It is where land values (the cost of land) are highest, because it is the most accessible part of the city. Only businesses that can afford high rents are located here.

2. Residential and industrial land use – as the city grows, a manufacturing zone consisting of industries and workers' houses develops around the centre. Housing here is cheap and near to jobs in factories. As the city continues to expand, this becomes the inner city, where housing may become run-down if industries close.

3. Industrial land use – as the city grows, industrial areas often expand along railway lines, major roads and canals leading into the city. Industries need good transport links for moving resources – these areas need to be accessible.

4. Residential land use – over time, as transport links improve, some people can afford to move out of the inner city to the suburbs. Land values are highest in the most sought-after areas – perhaps on hills overlooking the city.

5. As the city grows, people living in the suburbs have to commute for longer. Some people move back to the inner city and develop it.

6. Land use is also affected by planning regulations, which may prevent industrial land use in residential areas or residential land use on green belt land.

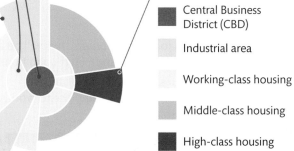

- Central Business District (CBD)
- Industrial area
- Working-class housing
- Middle-class housing
- High-class housing

Figure 1 An urban model showing land use

⑤ Worked example   Grades 5–7

Study **Figure 2**, which shows a regenerated inner city area in a developed country.

Figure 2 A regenerated area

Suggest **two** ways in which this area has changed over time.   **[4 marks]**

This is an inner-city area, so this building was probably once a factory. When the factory closed down because of deindustrialisation, the inner-city area became run-down and the population decreased. However, after many years, people wanted to move back to be near the city centre for work and leisure. This area was then regenerated, with new places to live (e.g. flats) and a cleaner, pleasant environment (e.g. pollution removed from the canal).

⑤ Key terms

- ☑ **Urbanisation:** an increase in the number of people living in cities
- ☑ **Suburbanisation:** the movement of people, industry and jobs from the centre of the city to its outer areas
- ☑ **Deindustrialisation:** the process of an area losing the industries that used to employ people there because production has moved to cheaper locations in other countries
- ☑ **Counter-urbanisation:** the movement of people out of the cities into the countryside
- ☑ **Regeneration:** new investment into old, run-down parts of the city (often inner-city areas)

① Exam-style practice   Grade 4

Which of the following is the movement of people and jobs away from the city centre to its outer areas?   **[1 mark]**

- ☐ **A** Urbanisation
- ☐ **B** Suburbanisation
- ☐ **C** Deindustrialisation
- ☐ **D** Counter-urbanisation

Megacity: Mumbai

You may need to answer a question about a megacity you have studied in a developing or emerging country. This case study looks at why the quality of life varies so much in Mumbai.

⑤ Case study

Location and importance of Mumbai

Figure 1 Mumbai has good transport links to the rest of India through its numerous rail and road networks.

- Mumbai is one of the most densely populated cities in the world. The **site** of a city is the land on which it is built. Mumbai was built on seven islands, meaning there was limited space for growth outwards.
- Mumbai contributes more than $300 billion to India's Gross Domestic Product (GDP). It is responsible for 25 per cent of India's industrial output and 70 per cent of its maritime trade.
- It has a range of industries, from textiles to petrochemicals, and serves as the headquarters for many companies, including the Reserve Bank of India. The Taloja industrial area is a hub for major industries such as chemical and pharmaceutical production.
- It is the base for the Bollywood film industry, which released over 300 films in 2016.
- The **situation** of a city is its position in relation to surrounding features. Mumbai is on the west coast of India (Arabian Sea). It has a busy port system and large stock exchanges which stimulate economic development across the region.

⑩ Population growth

You need to be able to explain how your case study city has grown. This will include knowing about the rate of natural increase in your city, migration, and reasons why people have migrated to the city. For Mumbai:

- 16 million people live in the city today, compared with 9.9 million in 1991.
- Mumbai's population is growing at a rate of 3 per cent per year. Half of this is because of migration and half is the result of natural increase.
- International migration contributes to the population growth. People move to Mumbai from around the world, attracted by the range of job opportunities.
- Nearly 70 per cent of migrants come from rural or urban areas within the surrounding Maharashtra state contributing to population growth. There is also a small amount of international migration from people seeking job opportunities.
- 1000 people arrive in Mumbai from elsewhere in India each day. Most of this migration is rural–urban migration.
- Most migrants to Mumbai are young people, who go on to have families in the city.

Migration
Pull factors:
- The city has a strong economy due to foreign investment, Bollywood and finance. It also has an important port and many manufacturing industries, especially textiles.
- There are many more social opportunities in the city than in rural areas, such as housing with access to electricity, better healthcare and better access to education.

Push factors:
- Low wages, poor healthcare and few educational opportunities in rural areas.
- Less demand for farm workers following improvements in agricultural technology.

⑩ Structure and changes

You need to be able to describe the **structure** of your megacity, including what its central business district (CBD) is like, the conditions in the inner city and the conditions in its suburbs. You should be able to link this to how your megacity has changed over time.

- The CBD is located in the oldest part of Mumbai, on the southern tip of the peninsula the city is situated on. The headquarters of transnational corporations (TNCs) such as Tata and Microsoft are located here, as well as Mumbai's financial district.
- Mumbai's first manufacturing industries were located in the CBD. When these industries relocated as the city grew and land value increased, the textile mills remained. Now these old buildings have been regenerated into extremely expensive flats.
- Mumbai's inner city is where the workers who once worked in the textile mills lived. This area is now very run-down and the workers' housing blocks are now slums. Squatter settlements, such as Dharavi, have grown here, typically along railway lines.
- Mumbai's outer suburbs stretch along its railway lines. A new suburb area called New Mumbai has been developed, and is much less congested. Industries, such as engineering, healthcare and IT, have relocated to New Mumbai as land is cheaper and costs are lower.

⑤ Exam-style practice   Grades 5–7

For a named megacity in a developing or emerging country, explain **two** pull factors that have attracted migrants to the city.   **[4 marks]**

Mumbai: Opportunities and challenges

You may need to answer a question about the opportunities and challenges for people living in your case study megacity. This case study is about Mumbai.

 ## Challenges caused by rapid growth

Providing clean water, sanitation systems and energy
Access to clean water is limited, with the use of standpipes restricted to two hours in the morning in some areas. There are many open sewers and polluted streams that pose a health risk. Millions of tonnes of waste are dumped into the Mithi River. There is limited access to energy resources, with supply not meeting the needs of the population.

Slums and squatter settlements
Squatter settlements have grown rapidly, expanding onto private land. They tend to be poorly constructed and overcrowded.

Reducing unemployment and crime
There is a shortage of skilled engineers and technicians and most people work in the 'informal sector', which often involves dangerous working conditions, no job security and poor pay.

Challenges of rapid urban growth in Mumbai

Traffic congestion
There are over 2 million cars in the city, causing gridlocked roads and increasing air pollution. The government is introducing a monorail to reduce the number of cars being used.

Health and education
Rapid population growth has resulted in increased pressure on the already strained health and education services available. Despite the growth of the Sion Hospital in Dharavi, many people still have to wait a long time to be treated.
Education is improving, but many schools are still overcrowded and there is a shortage of teachers.

Housing shortages The number of migrants arriving in Mumbai means that there are more people than there are places to live, leading to housing shortages.

 ## Worked example   Grades 5–7

For a named megacity in a developing or emerging country, explain **two** reasons why there are differences in quality of life in the megacity.   **[4 marks]**

In Mumbai, the main form of slum settlement is chawls. Chawls are extremely overcrowded and access to piped water is often limited, so there is a risk of disease spreading. Many wealthier citizens live in apartment blocks with clean running water and modern plumbing. Another reason for a difference in the quality of life is that in the chawls the quality of the housing is poor. These homes are often poorly constructed from scrap material and landlords may not have done repairs, so they are in danger of collapsing. The modern apartment blocks of the wealthy are built with higher standards of safety and quality of building materials. These homes are much more secure.

The command word 'explain' means that you need to give reasons for why or how something occurs.

 ## Opportunities in the megacity

- People come from all over the world to work in Mumbai's finance, IT and entertainment industries. These are well paid jobs for highly skilled people.
- Mumbai's growth has also created opportunities for low-skilled rural migrants. 68 per cent of Mumbai's residents work in the informal sector, in services such as transport, cleaning and small-scale manufacturing.
- Mumbai's slums and squatter settlements provide affordable housing for poor people and are located close to the wealthy areas of Mumbai.
- Access to more schools and healthcare resources provide more opportunities for education and quality of life than in many rural areas.

 ## Exam-style practice   Grades 4–6

For a named megacity in a developing or emerging country, explain **one** challenge caused by squatter and slum settlements.   **[3 marks]**

 Made a start   **Feeling confident**   **Exam ready**

Mumbai: Sustainability

You may need to answer a question about the advantages and disadvantages of strategies for making your case study megacity more sustainable. This case study is about Mumbai.

 What is a sustainable city?

In a sustainable city, people have a good quality of life but do not use up resources in a way that will cause people in the future to have a lower quality of life.

- Good public transport encourages people to use cars less. This reduces congestion and air pollution.
- Recycling water and waste prevents the city using up water supplies in its area and people having to deal with pollution.
- Making energy use as efficient and renewable as possible reduces carbon emissions and cuts down air pollution from city power plants.

 Worked example Grades 6–9

For a named megacity, assess the advantages and disadvantages of different strategies for making the megacity more sustainable. **[8 marks]**

Mumbai has unsustainable traffic congestion problems. The roads are clogged with vehicles, which causes air pollution. The city government decided to invest in a monorail. The monorail is above the roads, so it does not add to congestion, and it was built without having to relocate residents or businesses, which would be very difficult to do in Mumbai. Ticket prices were kept cheap so poorer people could use it to travel. However, the scheme has not been very successful so far because the routes go through industrial areas, even though local people usually travel from residential areas into the city centre. The limited success of the scheme may be ◄─── because local people were not involved enough in planning the routes for the monorail.

Mumbai's waste disposal is also unsustainable. In squatter settlements such as Dharavi, there are no sewers. About 500 people use each public latrine, so some people use streams and rivers running through the settlement instead. The city government provided toilet blocks for people to use, but the cost of using them was too expensive for poor families. An Indian NGO called SPARC worked with local communities using a different approach. People from the community built the blocks with the NGO's help. This was much more successful than the city government's strategy, because families from the community can use the blocks at any time for around 25p for a month. This is affordable for all families. So far 800 blocks have been built, each with eight toilets. However, Dharavi has 1 million inhabitants, so it will take some time to provide facilities for them all. This is the main disadvantage of this bottom-up strategy: it can only contribute to the megacity's sustainability on a small scale.

 Top-down strategies

Top-down sustainability strategies often come from city governments.

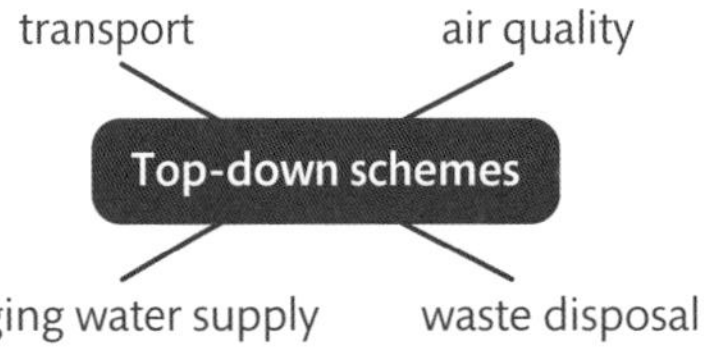

Figure 1 Types of top-down scheme

- 👍 City governments can access large budgets, so top-down projects can be on a large scale and benefit thousands of people.
- 👎 Large-scale projects can disrupt or even ruin life for many people.

> For 8-mark questions, you need to make judgements. This answer has described a strategy and why it was needed, and finished the paragraph by making a reasoned judgement.

 Bottom-up strategies

Bottom-up sustainability strategies are often led by local communities or non-governmental organisations (NGOs) such as charities.

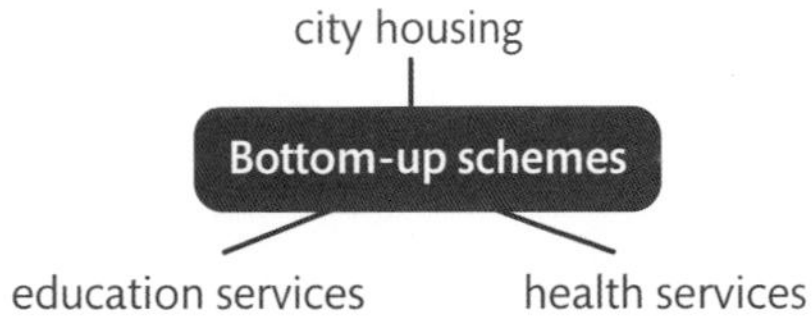

Figure 2 Types of bottom-up scheme

- 👍 Local communities have the opportunity to fix problems specific to them.
- 👎 Each bottom-up scheme only helps a small number of people.

 Exam-style practice Grades 5–7

For a named megacity, explain **two** ways in which a bottom-up scheme aims to make the megacity more sustainable. **[4 marks]**

 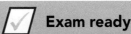

The UK's physical landscape

Geology and past tectonic and glacial processes have influenced the upland and lowland landscapes of the UK.

⑤ Rock groups ✓

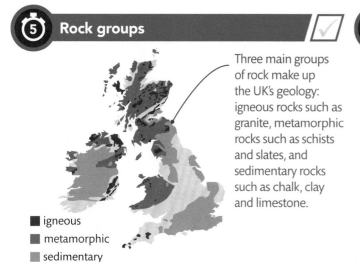

Three main groups of rock make up the UK's geology: igneous rocks such as granite, metamorphic rocks such as schists and slates, and sedimentary rocks such as chalk, clay and limestone.

■ igneous
■ metamorphic
■ sedimentary

Figure 1 A simplified map of the UK's geology

Rock type	Formation	Characteristics
Igneous	• Past tectonic processes created lava and magma, which solidified to form igneous rocks.	• Hard and made of crystals. • Mostly found in upland areas in the north of the UK.
Sedimentary	• Formed from sediments deposited on river beds or sea beds.	• Found mostly in lowland areas. • Some sedimentary rocks are very soft.
Metamorphic	• Existing rocks that have been changed by intense heating and compression.	• Harder and more resistant than other types of rock.

⑤ Worked example — Grades 4–6 ✓

Figure 4 A landscape in the Lake District

Describe how glaciation has affected the upland landscape in **Figure 4**. **[2 marks]**

A glacier has eroded away the rock on this mountain. Where the edge of the glacier was, the glacier has left a sharp ridge. Where the glacier began, it has left a deep lake.

⑤ Upland and lowland areas ✓

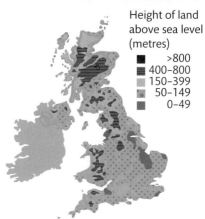

Height of land above sea level (metres)
■ >800
▥ 400–800
▦ 150–399
▨ 50–149
▤ 0–49

Figure 2 A relief map of the UK

Upland landscapes tend to have resistant igneous or metamorphic geology, whereas lowland landscapes tend to have less resistant sedimentary geology. Upland areas are located mostly in the north and west of the UK.

⑤ Glaciation ✓

Belfast · Edinburgh · Dublin · Nottingham · Cardiff · London
0 ___ 200 km ☐ Devensian ice sheet

Figure 3 Ice coverage during the Devensian period, the most recent glaciation, when ice stretched as far south as Cardiff

Both upland and lowland UK landscapes were affected by glaciation.

• Ice sheets covered upland UK areas during the last Ice Age and glaciers formed distinctive landscapes in places such as the Lake District.

• Lowland UK landscapes were affected, too. A lot of the land was covered in clay and debris, which was eroded by glaciers and washed down into lowland areas.

② Exam-style practice — Grade 5 ✓

Suggest **one** difference between metamorphic rocks and sedimentary rocks. **[2 marks]**

UK landscapes and rock groups

Different physical processes have acted together to help create upland and lowland landscapes in the UK.

(5) A granite upland landscape

Figure 1 shows a landform called a tor in the Dartmoor upland landscape.

- Dartmoor was formed by a huge dome of magma created deep underground 290 million years ago.
- The magma cooled to form granite, a resistant igneous rock. During the cooling, cracks formed. These cracks are called joints.
- Chemical weathering and freeze-thaw weathering widened the joints.
- Sections of granite with fewer joints were less weathered. They remain today as tors: towers of granite in the landscape.

Figure 1 Dartmoor, an upland landscape in Devon, in the south-west of the UK.

(10) A limestone upland landscape

Figure 2 Malham Cove, an upland carboniferous limestone landscape in Yorkshire, northern England.

Figure 2 shows Malham Cove, a larged curved limestone formation in the Yorkshire Dales National Park.

- Carboniferous limestone formed around 350 million years ago, when this part of Britain was covered by warm tropical seas.
- At the end of the last Ice Age, melting water from the glaciers formed a huge waterfall over the cliffs, eroding them back to create the cove.
- Since then, weathering and mass movement have continued to shape the landscape.
- At the top of the cliff is a limestone pavement, which is formed by chemical weathering of limestone.
- During the last Ice Age, ice left the limestone exposed and cracks in the rock were widened by rainwater, which gradually dissolves limestone (chemical weathering).

(10) A chalk escarpment lowland landscape

- Sedimentary rocks such as chalk and clay are formed in layers under different climate conditions.
- The layers were folded and tilted by plate tectonics. The clay was eroded more rapidly than the chalk to form valleys – called vales. As the clay is impermeable, streams and rivers form.
- The chalk creates escarpments – hills in the landscape with a steeper slope (called the scarp slope) and a gentler slope (the dip slope). These follow the line of the chalk layer.

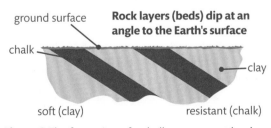

Figure 3 The formation of a chalk escarpment landscape

(2) Exam-style practice   Grade 5

Identify **one** landscape affected by chemical weathering processes.   **[1 mark]**

Landscapes and human activity

Agriculture, forestry and settlements have contributed to distinctive UK landscapes.

 ## Agricultural landscapes

Humans have altered all the landscapes of the UK through thousands of years of farming.

- Farming has cleared the land of its natural cover of temperate forest. In its place are fields.
- Fields are drained to make them better for growing crops. Drainage channels, shown on **Figure 1** as blue lines, are often straight.
- The UK's soils, relief and climate make the east of the country best for arable crops, including wheat. These lowland areas are flat. Fields here are often very large, to maximise efficiency from farm machinery.

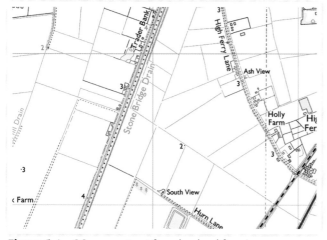

Figure 1 An OS map extract for a lowland farming area near Boston, Lincolnshire. The scale is 1:25 000.

Forestry

Forestry is growing trees and managing them in order to sell the wood.

- Because coniferous trees grow faster than deciduous trees, much commercial forestry uses conifer species such as the Sitka spruce.
- In the UK, upland areas have often been used for forestry. Mountain regions have steep relief, thin soils and colder climates, which are not good for farming crops. Forestry is a way of making money from this land.
- Upland areas are popular for outdoor leisure activities. People often associate forested areas with outdoor leisure. Trails for walkers, horse riders and cyclists are often made through forests.

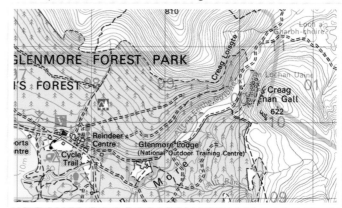

Figure 2 An OS map extract for a forested upland area in the Cairngorms National Park, Scotland. The scale is 1:50 000.

 ## Settlements

- Most settlements in the UK landscape have been there for many hundreds of years.
- The starting point for settlements was often a particular natural feature, such as a spring for water or a good defensive location.
- Houses and other buildings were made from local stone, so buildings in different areas would look distinctive because of changes in geology across the UK landscape.
- In modern times, local materials are not used so much for buildings. One result is that settlements in different parts of the UK landscape now look more similar to each other than they used to.

Figure 3 An old house made from flint – a rock associated with chalk landscapes.

 ## Exam-style practice — Grade 4

Analyse **Figure 1** and **Figure 2**, which show maps of lowland and upland areas. Suggest **one** reason why one of the locations is more suitable for arable farming than the other. **[2 marks]**

 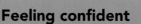

Coastal erosion landforms

Coastal erosion processes interact with rock type and rock structure to form distinctive landforms such as headlands and bays, cliffs and wave cut platforms, caves, arches and stacks.

(5) Coastal processes of erosion

- **Hydraulic action** (mechanical) – breaking waves compress pockets of air in cracks in a cliff. The increasing air pressure causes the cracks to widen, which leads to rocks breaking off.
- **Abrasion** (mechanical) – this is the action of rock fragments, carried by waves, being hurled at a cliff face, causing pieces of rock to chip off.
- **Attrition** (mechanical) – waves cause rocks and pebbles to collide with each other, causing them to become smaller and rounded.
- **Solution/Corrosion** (chemical) – acids and salts in seawater cause some rocks to gradually dissolve.

(5) Cliffs and wave cut platforms

1 Erosion creates a **wave cut notch** where waves crash against a cliff.

2 Continued erosion will cause the notch to increase in size, creating an **overhang**.

3 Eventually, the overhang will be unable to support itself and will collapse under the force of gravity.

4 As this process repeats itself, the cliff will retreat and leave a **wave cut platform**.

(5) Caves, arches and stacks

There are four stages in the formation of a stack.

1 Waves attack **joints** and **faults** (areas of weakness in the rock of a headland).

2 Over time, these areas of weakness increase in size to form a small **cave**.

3 If two caves form either side of the headland, eventually erosion will cause the backs of the caves to meet and break through, forming an **arch**.

4 The neck of the arch widens with additional erosion. This, along with weathering on the top, results in the arch collapsing, forming a **stack**. If a stack collapses it will leave a **stump**.

(2) Headlands and bays

Coastlines can be made up of alternating bands of hard, resistant rocks such as limestone, and soft, less resistant rocks such as clay. **Bays** are formed when the bands of less resistant rock erode. This leaves behind a band of more resistant rock jutting out into the sea. These are called **headlands**. As headlands jut out into the sea in this way, they are attacked by waves on three sides.

> For this question, you could have alternatively given abrasion or corrosion.

(2) Concordant and discordant coastline

Discordant coastlines have alternating bands of harder and softer rock perpendicular to the coast. The softer rocks are eroded more rapidly.

Concordant coastlines have the same type of rock along their length, and generally have fewer bays and headlands than discordant coastlines.

(2) Worked example — Grades 1–3

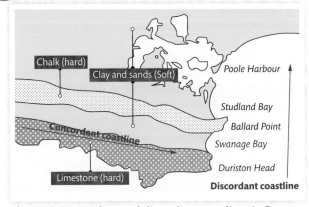

Figure 1 Concordant and discordant coastlines in Dorset

Study **Figure 1**, which shows an arch.
State **one** process of erosion that may affect this landform. **[1 mark]**

Hydraulic power

(10) Exam-style practice — Grades 4–7

1 Explain how coastal processes and geological structures interact to form a stack. **[4 marks]**

2 Using **Figure 1**, explain the differences between a discordant and concordant coastline. **[4 marks]**

Processes of coastal erosion

Many different factors affect coastal erosion in the UK, including the climate.

(5) Climate and waves

Waves are created by wind blowing over the surface of the sea. Different factors affect the strength of waves when they break on the coast, and whether they erode material (**destructive waves**) or deposit material (**constructive waves**).

- In the UK, **winds** are stronger in winter than in summer (seasonality). Stronger winds give waves more energy.
- **Storms** are more frequent in the UK in winter (seasonality). Powerful storm waves cause significant erosion.
- The **fetch** is how far a wave has travelled. Some waves have a very long fetch: waves affecting south-west Britain travel up to 4800 km across the Atlantic.
- **Prevailing winds** in the UK are from the south-west. Coasts facing south-west are most exposed.

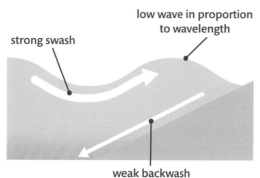

Figure 1 A constructive wave – common in summer when there is less wind and where prevailing winds have a short fetch.

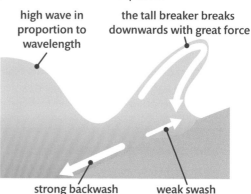

Figure 2 A destructive wave – occurs in winter storms and where prevailing winds have a long fetch.

(5) Types of weathering

Chemical weathering

When acidic rainwater falls on rocks, a chemical reaction can occur. Over time, this can cause certain rocks, such as limestone, to break down.

Mechanical weathering

Mechanical weathering includes several different physical processes of weathering, including cracking caused by the expansion and contraction of rocks as they heat up and cool down, the breakdown of trees by rocks (biological weathering), and **freeze-thaw** weathering.

Freeze-thaw weathering is a process in which rainwater falls into the cracks of rocks and freezes. This causes the water to expand, putting pressure on the rock. Repeated freezing and thawing causes the breakdown of rocks over time.

Exam focus

You can draw diagrams to answer questions like this if you find it quicker and easier.

(5) Worked example — Grades 4–6

The British Geological Survey (BGS) has been monitoring the rate of coastal retreat at Happisburgh in Norfolk, on the east coast of the UK. The coastline at Happisburgh is mostly made of sand and gravel. Between 1992 and 2004, 105 m of coastal retreat was measured.

1 Calculate the mean rate of coastal retreat in the 13 years from 1992 to 2004. Round your answer to the nearest whole number. **[1 mark]**

8 m

2 Explain **two** factors that contribute to high rates of coastal erosion. **[4 marks]**

If the coastline is exposed to waves with a long fetch, destructive waves will be more powerful and have more energy to erode the coast.

High rates of mechanical or chemical weathering could mean that rocks along the coast are weaker, and are more easily eroded by the sea.

(5) Exam-style practice — Grades 4–6

Explain **one** difference between destructive and constructive waves. **[2 marks]**

Made a start   Feeling confident   Exam ready

Mass movement and transportation

Surface materials move down a slope under the influence of gravity. This is known as **mass movement**. When mass movement occurs along coastlines, this material is often transported further along the coast by the process of **longshore drift**.

 ## Types of mass movement

Sliding

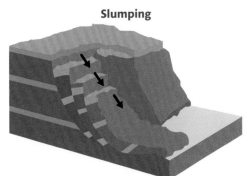

This is the sudden movement of large volumes of rock and soil along a zone of saturated soil.

Slumping

This is the mass movement of permeable rock and soil, such as clay, that has become heavily saturated, lying on top of impermeable material.

Rock falls

This is the free-fall movement of rock fragments due to gravity. This process is often increased by mechanical weathering.

Figure 1 Three types of mass movement

 ## Transport processes

Solution
dissolved minerals carried within the water

Traction
the rolling of large pebbles along the sea floor

Transport processes

Suspension
particles carried within the water

Saltation
the bouncing of small pebbles along the sea floor

 ## Worked example — Grade 5

Explain **one** way in which mass movement affects the rate of coastal erosion. **[2 marks]**

When cliffs are exposed to heavy rainfall or freeze-thaw weathering, it can cause the surface of the cliffs to become unstable and collapse causing a landslide, for example. Landslides could contribute to further cliff retreat.

 ## Longshore drift

Longshore drift is the gradual movement of sediment along the coast. The direction of the prevailing wind causes the waves to approach the beach at an oblique angle (swash) and return at a right angle (backwash). This causes sediment to be carried along the coast in a zigzag.

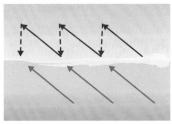

- – backwash
— swash
— prevailing wind

Figure 2 Longshore drift

Give specific details about the process you are explaining.

Use relevant key terms in your explanation.

 ## Exam-style practice — Grades 2–4

1. State **one** type of mass movement. **[1 mark]**

2. Describe **one** way slumping affects coastal landscapes. **[2 marks]**

 Made a start   **Feeling confident**   **Exam ready**

Coastal deposition landforms

Longshore drift and constructive waves influence coastal landforms that are formed by deposition: beaches, spits and bars.

 Beaches, spits and bars

Beaches

Beaches form from the deposition of material by waves. Low-energy constructive waves create **sandy beaches**. Sandy beaches are generally shallow or flat in gradient. They are often found in bays where the water is shallow and the waves have less energy. High-energy destructive waves create **shingle (pebble) beaches** as the backwash is stronger. Shingle beaches generally have a steep gradient. They are found where cliffs are being eroded and the waves have more energy.

Spits

A **spit** is a narrow accumulation of sand and shingle formed by longshore drift, which is caused by the prevailing wind blowing at an angle to the coastline. One end of a spit is connected to land and the other end projects out into the sea.

1. Sediment is carried by longshore drift.

2. Where the coastline changes shape, the waves lose energy, so the sediment is deposited. Over time, it accumulates to form a spit.

4. A **salt marsh** forms from the build-up of deposited sediments behind the spit.

3. Strong **secondary winds** cause the end of the spit to curve.

Figure 1 Spurn Head, East Yorkshire

Bars

A bar forms if a spit extends across a bay, connecting to a headland on the other side. This results in the formation of a **lagoon**, which is a saltwater lake.

 Worked example **Grades 5–7**

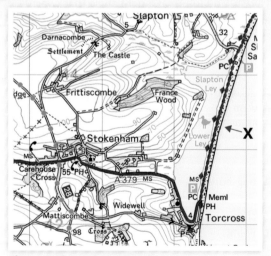

Figure 2 The scale is 1:50000

Study **Figure 2**, a 1:50000 scale Ordnance Survey extract showing part of the Devon coastline in south-west England.

Explain how feature **X** was formed. **[4 marks]**

1. Longshore drift moves sediment along the coast in the direction of the prevailing wind.

2. Where the coastline changes direction, such as at the Torcross headland on Figure 2, longshore drift continues to push sediment out into the sea. The flow of a river or stream from a bay out into the sea can create low-energy conditions in which deposition takes place.

3. A spit develops. If the flow of the river or stream is not strong enough to erode through the spit, then the spit grows right across the bay and forms a bar.

4. Behind the bar, sediment carried down by the stream or river builds up and a lagoon forms.

Numbering the steps in a process makes your answer clear. You can also number stages in a diagram.

 Exam-style practice **Grade 4**

1 State **two** differences between constructive and destructive waves. **[2 marks]**

2 Using **Figure 2**, suggest how the area may be affected by rising sea levels in the future. **[2 marks]**

 Made a start **Feeling confident** **Exam ready**

Human activities in coastal landscapes

Human activity can also affect coastal landscapes. Sometimes these activities can interact with physical processes and sometimes they can work against them.

10 Types of activity

Development	Agriculture	Industry

Figure 1 A densely populated coastal city	**Figure 2** Farmland on the coast	**Figure 3** A power station on the coast
• One billion humans worldwide live on the coast. Coasts are increasingly developed. • Developed land needs protection from erosion and coastal flooding. • Development interrupts coastal processes, such as the transfer of sediment along the coast.	• More sediment goes into the sea as water and wind erode soil from ploughed fields near the coast. • Coastal erosion and flooding threaten farmland. • Farmers can use coastal fields for other purposes, for example, renting them out as caravan parks.	• Industries that use a lot of water, such as power production, often locate on the coast. • Industry conflicts with tourism when industrial buildings and pollution spoil the natural landscape of coasts. • Power industries need protection from coastal erosion and flooding.

5 Coastal management

The coastal landscape is very dynamic, which means it is always changing. When humans develop the coastal landscape, this development needs either to work with physical processes or try to prevent those processes from changing the coast. For example:

• Beach replenishment **works with** physical processes by adding more sediment to replace that transported by longshore drift.

• Groynes **work against** physical processes as they block the transport of sediment along a beach.

5 Worked example   Grades 5–7

Figure 4 Hornsea, Yorkshire, UK

Study **Figure 4**, an aerial photograph of Hornsea, Yorkshire, UK.

Explain **two** ways in which human activity has had a direct impact on the coastal landscape.   **[4 marks]**

Figure 4 shows that groynes have been used to block longshore drift. This has changed the width of the beach as sediment has built up behind each groyne. This could help reduce erosion of the land behind the beach as a wider beach reduces wave energy.

This coastline has also been developed: the image shows housing along the land above the beach. The weight of the houses could make slopes less stable. This could have an impact on mass movement along the coastline.

1 Exam-style practice   Grade 4

Using **Figure 4**, explain **one** enquiry question you could investigate by fieldwork on this stretch of coastline. **[2 marks]**

The changing Holderness coast

You need to know an example of how human and physical processes are causing change in one named coastal landscape. This page looks at the Holderness coast in Yorkshire.

 Named example

The Holderness coastline, East Yorkshire

Figure 1 The Holderness coastline, East Yorkshire, is being eroded rapidly at an average of 1–2 metres a year.

 Worked example **Grades 4–6**

Figure 2 Coastal cliff, Yorkshire, UK

Study **Figure 2**, which shows a cliff at Hornsea on the Holderness coast.

This cliff is vulnerable to slumping. Explain the mass movement process of slumping. **[4 marks]**

Slumping is when a whole section of cliff slides downwards. It often happens where cliffs are made of soft clay overlying a harder rock, such as chalk. When rain saturates the clay, it makes it heavier and unstable. It can then slide off the layer beneath it. Waves undercutting the cliff can also make slumping more likely to happen.

 Change on the Holderness coast

Physical processes

- The coast is made of soft boulder clay, which is easily eroded. It also slumps when saturated.
- Powerful North Sea storms in winter cause destructive waves, resulting in rapid erosion of the unconsolidated boulder clay cliffs.
- Strong prevailing winds power longshore drift, which transports eroded sediment southwards along the coast. The spit at Spurn Head (**Figure 1**) is evidence of longshore drift. It protects important shipping channels along the Humber Estuary from silting up.
- Coastal defences north of Spurn Head that block longshore drift could cause the spit to become eroded if too little sediment reaches it.

Human processes

Farmland and housing are threatened by coastal retreat. Some locations have been protected with hard engineering. For example, the village of Mappleton has been protected from cliff erosion with two rock groynes and rock armour. Rock armour uses boulders to reduce wave energy.

However, the hard engineering at Mappleton has reduced the amount of sediment that is transported further down the coast. This may have increased erosion at locations south of Mappleton, such as the village of Aldborough, as beaches become narrower and give less protection to cliffs.

Human activities can cause positive changes to coastal areas. Management strategies that work with natural processes, such as managed retreat, can create valuable wildlife habitats. Spurn Head is an important nature reserve for seabirds.

Exam-style practice **Grades 6–9**

Describe **two** ways human activities are causing change on a named coastal landscape. **[2 marks]**

Go to page 39 to revise slumping.

Coastal flooding

Climate change is increasing the risk of coastal flooding and its threats to people and to the environment.

⑩ Causes of coastal flooding

Coastal flooding happens when low-lying land at the coast that is not usually covered by high tides is flooded with seawater. Coastal flooding most frequently happens because of storm surges.

- Very powerful storm winds create large waves, which push seawater onto the land.
- The very low-pressure weather conditions of storms 'pull' the sea level up, so that it floods into low-lying areas.
- Storm surges often occur when a powerful storm happens at the same time as a spring tide. This is when high tides are at their highest.

  Spring tides happen twice per month, not just in spring.

Figure 1 Areas in England and Wales most at risk of coastal flooding are shown in red.

⑤ Threats to people and the environment

- People can be killed if they are trapped in a flood. In 1953, over 300 people were killed by a storm surge in the UK. 1800 people in the Netherlands were killed by flooding from the same storm.
- Housing and businesses can be damaged or destroyed by coastal flooding. For example, in 2013 Storm Xaver led to coastal flooding of 2800 houses on the east coast of the UK. 18000 people had to be evacuated or rescued. Industries by the coast can lose power. Farmland that is flooded can become unusable because of the salt from the seawater.
- The power of storm surges accelerates coastal erosion. Storm surges can sometimes destroy, overnight, coastal landforms that have taken thousands of years to form.
- Climate changes poses an economic threat. In 2014, a winter storm swept away part of a sea wall protecting a railway line at Dawlish in Devon. Repairing the railway and sea wall cost £35 million.

⑤ Climate change

- Warmer sea temperatures increase the frequency and strength of storms. (See page 6 to see how this works with tropical cyclones, which are extreme low-pressure storms). More frequent and more powerful storms make it more likely that a storm surge will occur.
- Water expands when it warms and warmer global temperatures mean ice on the land is melting. These two processes are causing sea levels to rise. A global sea level rise of 7 cm has been measured over the last 25 years. Levels could rise by 60 cm by 2100.
- 2.5 million people are already at risk of coastal flooding in the UK today. The UK is one of the European countries most vulnerable to coastal flooding.
- By 2100 sea levels around the UK could have risen by as much as 80 cm.
- By the end of the 21st century, 7000 UK properties are likely to be lost to increased coastal erosion linked to climate change – with 800 being lost in the next 20 years.

Figure 2 The railway at Dawlish is vulnerable to rapid erosion from coastal flooding.

⑤ Exam-style practice   Grades 4–6

Suggest **two** ways in which coastal flooding might threaten human activities.   **[4 marks]**

✓ **Made a start**   ✓ **Feeling confident**   ✓ **Exam ready**

Coastal management options

Managing coastal processes is difficult. The most effective protection is usually the most expensive to install and maintain, and the least sustainable management option.

 ## Costs and benefits

Hard engineering		
Method	**Benefits**	**Costs**
Groynes Groynes are barriers that stretch out into the sea at right angles, preventing longshore drift from removing sediment from the beach.	• Groynes widen the beach, providing more protection from storm erosion. • Wider beaches are popular with tourists.	• Groynes prevent sediment reaching beaches further down the coast, increasing their vulnerability to erosion. • Groynes can cost from £10 000 to £100 000 depending on size. • Groynes are unattractive.
Sea walls These are concrete walls that protect cliffs from erosion. They are often curved to reflect wave energy back into the sea.	• Sea walls prevent erosion very effectively as long as they are repaired regularly. • Walkways along the top of sea walls are popular.	• Sea walls are very expensive to construct at £2000 per metre. • If they are not maintained, they will eventually be eroded.
Soft engineering		
Method	**Benefits**	**Costs**
Beach replenishment Sediment is added to a beach in order to replace sediment lost by longshore drift.	• More sand makes the beach more effective at reducing erosion by storms. • Larger beaches are popular with tourists.	• Sand has to be replaced frequently. • It costs around £3000 per km. • Sediment is often pumped from off shore, damaging marine ecosystems.
Slope stabilisation Drains are added to slopes to reduce the risk of slumping and mesh is added to keep slopes in place.	• Slope stabilisation makes beaches under cliffs safer for tourists. • Slopes are made more resistant to mass movement.	• Installing drainage can be expensive and disruptive. • Slope stabilisation does not prevent wave erosion at the slope base.

 ## Sustainable management

Although soft engineering works with physical processes more than hard engineering does, soft engineering still has to be regularly repaired, renewed or replaced.

The most sustainable management methods do not interfere with physical processes.

- **Strategic realignment** is when the coastline is allowed to erode in ways that create natural defences to erosion, such as salt marshes. Salt marsh is a valuable wildlife habitat, is good at absorbing wave energy and is not damaged by coastal flooding.
- The '**do nothing**' approach is when no further action is taken to defend a coastline or relocate property.

Integrated Coastal Zone Management

Integrated Coastal Zone Management involves creating shoreline management plans (SMPs) for different sections of coastline. For each section, SMPs decide whether to:

1 advance the existing defence line

2 hold the existing defence line

3 carry out strategic realignment

4 'do nothing' (carry out no active intervention).

Worked example — Grades 4–6

Suggest **one** reason why people living on the same coastline may have conflicting views about Integrated Coastal Zone Management. **[2 marks]**

Farmers may object to losing grazing land because of strategic realignment, but birdwatchers might be positive about new habitats for wading birds.

 ## Exam-style practice — Grades 5–7

Look at **Figure 4** on page 41 which shows groynes at Hornsea, Yorkshire. Explain why this type of sea defence has been used here. **[3 marks]**

River landscapes

As a river moves through its upper, middle and lower courses there are changes in its profile and channel shape, in its velocity (speed), discharge and other factors.

 15 **River characteristics**

The **long profile** shows how a river's gradient changes as it flows from the source to the mouth.

The **cross profile** shows how the cross-sectional shape of the river bed changes.

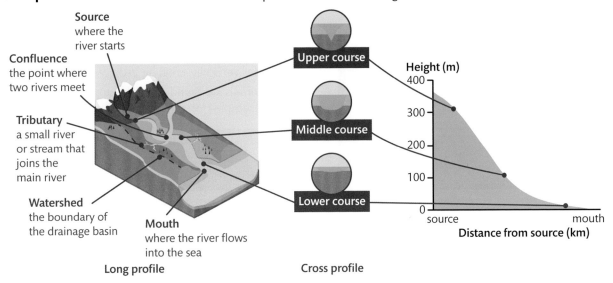

Figure 1 The long and cross profiles of a river

Changing river characteristics

Upper course	Middle course	Lower course
• River channel is narrow and shallow.	• The gradient is less steep.	• The gradient is very gentle.
• This reduces the discharge and energy of the river.	• Because the load has been transported along the river bed, it has become smaller and more rounded.	• The channel has become wide, deep and more U-shaped.
• The bedload is large and very angular.		• The bedload is now fine sediment.
• As the gradient is steep, the main type of erosion is vertical erosion, creating a V-shaped valley and a V-shaped channel.	• This increases the discharge and energy of the river, creating more lateral erosion and a wider and deeper channel.	• The discharge is very high.
		• When the river floods, sediment (alluvium) is deposited along the side of the river banks, forming a wide, flat floodplain made up of fertile alluvium.

— The bedload is the sediment that the river is transporting along its bed.

 5 **Worked example** **Grades 4–6**

Explain why the channel shape of a river changes as it flows downstream. **[4 marks]**

The source of a river is often on high land with steeper slopes. As the river flows over this land, it erodes vertically through hydraulic action, abrasion and attrition, leading to steep-sided V-shaped valleys and narrow, shallow river channels. The volume of water running through the channel (discharge) increases further downstream, partly due to the increased volume of water as tributaries join the river. This increased discharge, as well as increased velocity, leads to increased energy. Vertical erosion becomes less significant, and lateral erosion and deposition become more significant. This creates wider and deeper channels and wider and flatter valleys. In the lower course of the river, the surrounding land is flat, the river's energy is low and deposition is more dominant than erosion.

 5 **Exam-style practice** **Grades 4–6**

Explain why sediment size and shape change along the course of a river. **[4 marks]**

 Made a start **Feeling confident** 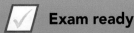 **Exam ready**

The course of the River Severn

You need to know about the changes taking place along the course of a UK river. This page uses the example of the River Severn.

Named example

The River Severn

Source: Plynlimon, Wales

Passes through: Powys, Shropshire, Worcestershire, Gloucestershire

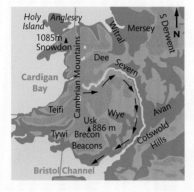

Key facts:

- It is the largest river in Great Britain.
- It flows for 220 miles from the Welsh mountains to the Bristol Channel.
- Its estuary is home to over 80 species of fish.

Upper course

The upper course is in the mountains of Wales.

- The steep slopes are mostly made of hard, impermeable slates and shales.
- The river profile gradient here is steep and the river erodes vertically, creating V-shaped valleys.
- Waterfalls are found along the upper course, for example Horseshoe Falls in Brecon.

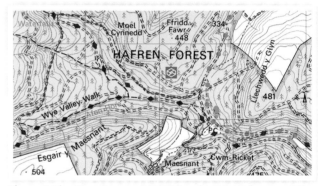

Figure 1 The River Severn. 1:50000 scale. Extract from an OS map.

Middle course

- As more tributaries, such as the River Avon, join the Severn, its discharge increases.
- The river channel becomes wider and deeper.
- As the gradient of the river's profile becomes gentler, the river erodes sideways through lateral erosion, making the valley wider and flatter, and creating areas of flood plain.

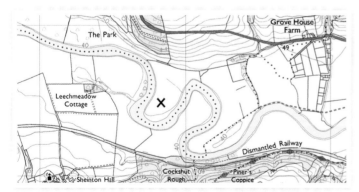

Figure 2 The River Severn. 1:25000 scale. Extract from an OS map.

Lower course

- The lower course of the River Severn is mainly over soft clays, sands and gravels.
- The river channel widens; 200 m wide at some points.
- The river's velocity is highest in the lower course because the smooth, deep and wide channel produces little friction.
- The river transports a lot of sediment. It deposits this in the lower course, especially close to the mouth of the river, where tides coming in from the sea decrease its velocity.

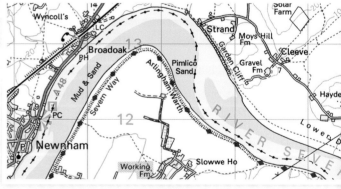

Figure 3 The River Severn. 1:50000 scale. Extract from an OS map.

Exam-style practice   Grades 1–3

1. Study **Figure 2**. Identify landform X.   **[1 mark]**
2. Using **Figure 3**, explain how you can determine that the river is in its lower course.   **[2 marks]**

River processes

River processes include erosion, which is the sculpting and wearing away of the landscape, transportation, which is the movement of sediment within the river channel, and deposition.

Erosion

Types of erosion

There are two key types of erosion that occur at different stages of a river:

- **vertical** erosion (occurring downwards)
- **lateral** erosion (occurring sideways).

Processes of erosion

A river's **load** is the material it carries. The load is used to erode rock.

- **Hydraulic action** – The force of the river hitting the banks and river bed can cause air to become trapped in cracks. The increasing pressure causes the banks to weaken and wear away.
- **Abrasion** – Rock fragments carried by the river hit the banks and the bed, causing them to wear down.
- **Attrition** – Rock fragments transported by the river collide, which causes them to break into smaller, more rounded sediment.
- **Solution** – Rocks containing calcium carbonate (e.g. limestone) react with slightly acidic river water to form a solution.

Transportation and deposition

Transportation

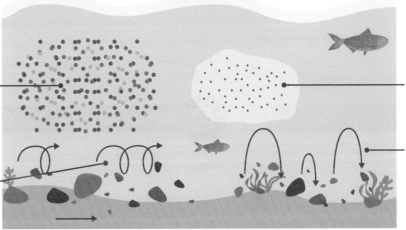

Suspension particles carried within the water

Solution dissolved minerals carried within the water

Saltation the bouncing of small pebbles along the river bed

Traction the rolling of large pebbles along the river bed

Figure 1 Transportation processes

Deposition

Deposition occurs when the energy of a river decreases and it is no longer able to transport its load. This can happen when the river meets another body of water at the river mouth or where the water is shallower, such as on the inside of a bend.

Worked example — Grades 1–2

Which of the following describes the process of attrition? **[1 mark]**

- [ ] **A** The dissolving of rocks such as limestone by a river.
- [✗] **B** The action of rocks colliding into each other.
- [ ] **C** The sheer force of water hitting the bed and banks of a channel.
- [ ] **D** When rocks wear away the river bed and banks.

Option **A** describes the process of solution and option **C** could describe the process of hydraulic action or abrasion, so option **B** is the correct answer.

Exam-style practice — Grades 2–4

1 Name **one** process of river transportation. **[1 mark]**

2 Explain why hydraulic action and abrasion may affect river channel shape. **[4 marks]**

River erosion landforms

In the upper course of a river, vertical erosion from processes such as hydraulic action is dominant. This leads to the formation of waterfalls, gorges and interlocking spurs.

 Formation of waterfalls and gorges

 hard rock   soft rock

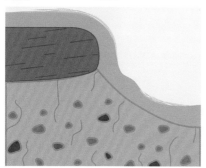

Waterfalls usually form in the upper course of a river where water flows over a band of hard rock that overlies a band of soft rock.

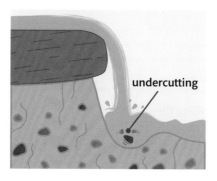

As the river flows over waterfalls, it forms a plunge pool due to the hydraulic action of the water weakening the soft rock. The erosion processes of hydraulic action and abrasion interact to undercut the soft rock and create an overhang.

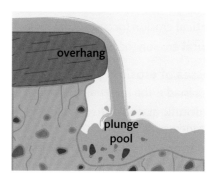

Over time, the overhang is unable to support itself and it collapses under the force of gravity. The rocks get trapped in the plunge pool further eroding the soft rock and deepening the plunge pool.

Figure 1 Waterfalls form where hard rock lies over soft rock.

The process shown in **Figure 1** repeats over centuries, causing the **waterfall** to retreat upstream and form a steep-sided valley. This is known as a **gorge**.

 Interlocking spurs

Interlocking spurs form as the river flows around the areas of hard rock, finding the easiest route.

Named example

Figure 2 Interlocking spurs in Carding Mill Valley in the Shropshire Hills.

 Worked example   **Grades 5–7**

Explain the processes involved in the formation of a gorge.   **[4 marks]**

Gorges can be formed by erosion as a waterfall retreats up a valley. This happens when a river flows over a band of hard, resistant rock that lies over the top of softer, less resistant rock. The river erodes the softer rock faster, through the processes of hydraulic action and abrasion. This erosion leads to the undercutting of the softer rock. Over time, continued erosion causes an overhang of the hard rock to form. Eventually, the harder rock is unable to support itself and collapses, deepening the plunge pool and creating a steep drop between the top of the waterfall and the bottom. This process repeats, causing the waterfall to retreat upstream and leave behind a steep and narrow gorge.

Describe the steps of the process and reference physical processes such as hydraulic action.

 Exam-style practice   **Grades 3–4**

Describe **one** factor that can cause a gorge to form.   **[2 marks]**

     Made a start   **Feeling confident**   **Exam ready**

River erosion and deposition landforms

Deposition occurs when a river no longer has enough energy to transport its load. The accumulation of these deposits combine, which results in the formation of a variety of different landforms.

⑤ Meanders ✓

- **Meanders** are found in the middle to lower course of a river where the land is flatter.
- The water flows from shallow to deep creating helicoidal flow (i.e. it flows in a corkscrew pattern).
- The line of fastest flow in the river moves to the outside of the bend and causes lateral erosion creating a **river cliff**.
- On the inside of the bend where the flow is slower and there is more friction, material is deposited to form a **slip-off slope**.
- The combination of lateral erosion and deposition causes meanders to move and change shape.

⑤ Oxbow lakes ✓

▨ areas of deposition
▧ areas of erosion

Erosion can cause both sides of a meander to migrate towards each other.

The neck becomes narrower and eventually the river breaks through.

Deposition occurs at the ends of the old meander loop

This forms a straighter channel and an oxbow lake.

Figure 1 Oxbow lakes form from meanders.

⑤ Deposition landforms ✓

- A **floodplain** is a wide, flat area of land on either side of a river that is often subject to flooding. Floodplains are caused by the migration of meanders due to lateral erosion. The resulting low-lying floodplain is covered with fine sediment and alluvium that is deposited when a river floods.
- A **levée** is an elevated bank along a river's edge. It forms when repeated flooding leads to deposition. The heaviest sediment is deposited first, as the river loses energy, and finer sediment (**alluvium**) is deposited further from the river.

Deltas

Deltas are wide plains of sediment that form where a river deposits sediment more quickly than currents and waves can carry it away. They are found in the lower course, at a river's mouth, where it flows into a lake or sea.

There are normally three types of deposit that form deltas.

① As a river's velocity decreases, the biggest, heaviest sediments are deposited first. These create topset beds.

② Medium-sized sediments form the foreset beds, and are carried further before being deposited.

③ The smallest, lightest sediments are carried furthest into the sea or lake and form bottomset beds when they are deposited.

As sediment is deposited to form the delta, the river splits into many smaller streams over a wide area.

⑤ Worked example   Grades 5–8 ✓

Identify the landform that is characteristic of the middle course of a river.   **[1 mark]**

☐ **A** Deltas

☐ **B** Interlocking spurs

☒ **C** Oxbow lakes

☐ **D** Floodplain

⑩ Exam-style practice   Grades 5–8 ✓

Explain the processes involved in the formation of meanders.   **[4 marks]**

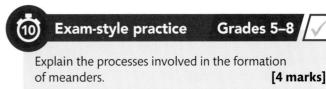

Storm hydrographs

Storm hydrographs help scientists predict flooding patterns by showing how varying levels of precipitation affect a river during a storm. Precipitation is moisture that falls to the ground, such as rain, snow, sleet or hail.

⑮ Storm hydrographs

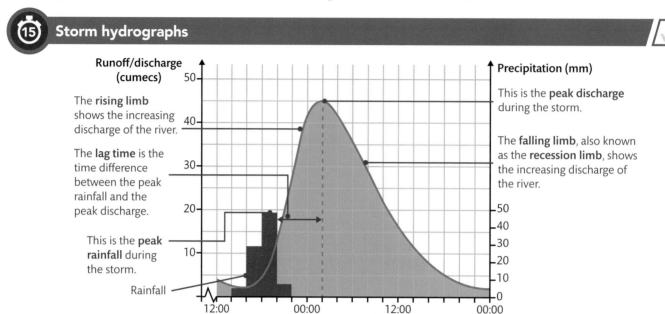

Runoff/discharge (cumecs)

The **rising limb** shows the increasing discharge of the river.

The **lag time** is the time difference between the peak rainfall and the peak discharge.

This is the **peak rainfall** during the storm.

Rainfall

Precipitation (mm)

This is the **peak discharge** during the storm.

The **falling limb**, also known as the **recession limb**, shows the increasing discharge of the river.

Time (hours)

Figure 1 A storm hydrograph is composed of a bar chart showing precipitation and a line graph showing the discharge of a river. The discharge of a river is the volume of water passing a particular point each second. It is measured in cumecs — cubic metres per second.

Factors affecting storm hydrographs

Hydrographs can be different shapes, depending upon the characteristics of a river and how likely it is to flood.

- A **flashy hydrograph** indicates that the river is more at risk of flooding. Flashy hydrographs have a steep rising limb, indicating the discharge of the river is increasing rapidly, and a short lag time, showing rainwater reaches the river quickly. Sustained heavy rainfall, steep slopes, clay soil and impermeable rock can all contribute to a short lag time and a flashy hydrograph.

- A **gentle hydrograph** shows that a river is less at risk of flooding. Gentle hydrographs have a long lag time and a less steep rising limb, indicating that rain water is taking longer to reach the channel, so the river discharge is increasing slowly. Lighter, intermittent rainfall, gentle slopes, well-drained soil and permeable rock all result in a longer lag time and a gentle hydrograph.

⑤ Worked example   Grades 4–6

Explain how geology can affect the shape of a storm hydrograph.   **[4 marks]**

If the land surrounding the river consists of lots of impermeable rocks, such as granite, there will be less infiltration of water and therefore increased surface runoff. This causes the water to reach the river channel much faster, so the discharge increases more quickly, creating a flashy hydrograph with a steep rising limb. However, if the surrounding land consists of permeable rocks, water will infiltrate the rocks, increasing groundwater flow, so the rate at which the water reaches the channel is slower. This creates a gentle hydrograph with a less steep rising limb representing a longer lag time.

When estimating the lag time, find the difference between the peak discharge and the peak rainfall.

Describe the appearance of the hydrograph for a small drainage basin and for a large drainage basin, giving reasons for the different shapes.

⑩ Exam-style practice   Grades 3–5

1 Study **Figure 1**. Calculate the lag time.   **[1 mark]**

2 Explain how precipitation can affect the shape of a flood hydrograph.   **[4 marks]**

Factors affecting storm hydrographs

Different physical factors and human activities change the way river landscapes respond to rainfall, which results in different storm hydrographs.

15 Physical factors

Differences in storm hydrographs and lag times can be explained by the effect of different physical factors.

1 **Size of drainage basin**: In small drainage basins, rainfall reaches the river channel quickly but discharge is lower than in a large drainage basin. In a large drainage basin, it takes longer for rainfall to reach the river but much more rainfall enters the river overall.

2 **Vegetation**: Bare soil or little vegetation means there is more **surface runoff**, which creates a flashy hydrograph. Lots of vegetation, for example in wooded or forested areas, means higher amounts of **interception** and plant roots help **infiltration**, so the hydrograph is gentler.

3 **Valley side steepness**: Steep slopes produce rapid runoff and a flashy hydrograph, while gentler slopes produce slower surface runoff and a gentle hydrograph.

4 **Soil type**: When soil is already **saturated** by previous rainfall, when soils are **impermeable** or when the soil is frozen, less water infiltrates the soil and more runs off. Permeable soils, such as sandy soils, and dry soils allow much more water to infiltrate, producing gentle hydrographs.

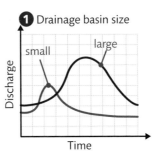
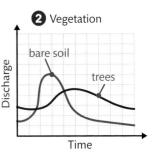
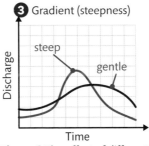
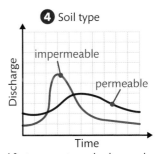

Figure 1 The effect of different physical factors on storm hydrographs

Antecedent conditions

If a lot of rain has already saturated the soil before a storm event or if cold weather has frozen the soil before a storm event, these **antecedent conditions** will influence how the drainage basin responds to a rain storm.

2 Worked example Grades 4–6

Figure 1 shows the effects of different physical factors on storm hydrographs.

Suggest how climate change could affect a storm hydrograph. **[3 marks]**

Climate change could make the UK's climate warmer, which could create more evaporation and wetter conditions. This could mean that river discharge may increase. There could also be more extreme weather events, with more storms and heavy rain, which could cause peak discharge to increase.

5 Human activity

Human activities can change river landscapes so that they respond differently to storm events.

- Urbanisation creates more impermeable surfaces, increasing runoff. Drains also transfer water into river channels more quickly.
- Deforestation reduces interception and infiltration, increasing surface runoff. Compacting soil, for example by machinery, also reduces infiltration and increases runoff.
- Changes in land use can affect runoff. For example, afforestation increases interception and infiltration. Growing crops increases runoff, especially when furrows go down a slope rather than across it.

2 Exam-style practice Grades 4–6

Explain **one** reason why a deforested area near a river is more likely to produce a flashy hydrograph than an area with dense vegetation. **[2 marks]**

River flooding risks

Changes in climate and land use are causing risks from river flooding to increase. You should know an example of a river where flooding has taken place.

Increased risks

Growing demands for housing mean that floodplains are used for residential developments. This changes the land use and increases the number of people at risk from flooding.

- short periods of intense rainfall during storms can lead to flooding and storms are becoming more frequent.
- warmer temperatures mean there is more energy in the atmosphere, making storms more powerful.
- warmer temperatures increase evaporation from seas and lakes, increasing water vapour/precipitation.
- climate change may also change weather patterns, bringing more rain to some areas.

Physical and human processes

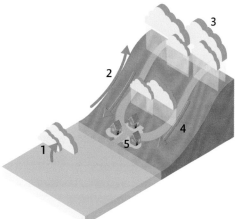

Figure 1 Processes causing flooding at Cockermouth

1. Storm Desmond hit the UK on 4–6 December 2015.
2. Warm, moist air was forced up over the mountains of Cumbria (the Lake District).
3. As the air cooled, the water vapour condensed to form rain. The weather front (depression) then stopped over Cumbria. In one upland area, 341.1 mm of rain fell in 24 hours, breaking previous UK rainfall records. Extreme weather events like this are often seen as a sign of climate change.
4. Antecedent conditions meant that the ground was already saturated, so the heavy rain ran over the surface, down the steep slopes and into the rivers.
5. The existing flood defences at the town of Cockermouth were not sufficient to hold back the volume of water in the rivers. Severe flooding took place at Cockermouth, at the confluence of the Rivers Derwent and Cocker.

Threats to people and the environment

Social
Effects on people can include:
- sustaining injuries
- damage to property.

Economic
Effects on the wealth of an area can include:
- reduced tourism
- the cost of repairs and restoration.

Environmental
Effects on the surrounding landscape can include:
- destruction of crops
- loss of livestock.

Named example

River flooding at Cockermouth, 2015
Location: Cumbria, north-west England
Physical causes of flooding: Extremely heavy rainfall from Storm Desmond and already saturated ground. The rain poured into the River Derwent and the River Cocker from the steep mountain slopes.
Human causes of flooding: The location of the town at the confluence of two rivers, the River Derwent and the River Cocker, increased the risk of flooding. Cockermouth had been flooded before, for example in 2005 and 2009. Flood defences were inadequate: a flood barrier was constructed there in 2013, but the flooding caused by Storm Desmond was higher than the barrier.

Worked example — Grades 4–6

Explain what is meant by the term **antecedent conditions**. [2 marks]

Antecedent conditions are the conditions before a storm event that influence the response of the drainage basin to the storm. For example, if soils are already saturated with water from previous rainfall, or if rivers are already swollen with water from previous rainfall or snowmelt.

Exam-style practice — Grades 5–7

Explain how physical processes have contributed to a flood event on **one** named river. [4 marks]

 Made a start   Feeling confident   Exam ready

Managing flood risk

Hard engineering and soft engineering both have costs and benefits.

 Costs and benefits of management methods

Hard engineering method	Benefits	Costs
Flood walls are artificial barriers used to raise the height of river banks. They are often made of concrete and brick, sometimes with glass panels.	• The river can hold more water before flooding. • Flood walls can be made of glass, or move up as river levels rise, so they don't block views.	• Long flood walls are very expensive to build and maintain. • They are not effective if the river rises higher than the barrier.
Embankments are high banks built on top of or near natural river banks. They are made of earth and covered with grass.	• The river can hold more water before flooding. • Embankments are cheaper to build than flood walls, and easier to repair.	• Floodwater can burst through weak points. It can then get trapped behind the banks.
Temporary flood barriers are temporary structures, put up when river flooding is predicted to protect areas that are at risk.	• Temporary barriers can be used in scenic urban locations where a permanent flood wall would look ugly.	• Temporary barriers must be deployed (set up) in time to be useful. • Can cause flooding downstream.
Permanent flood barriers are floodgates built near the river mouth to prevent storm surges from flooding urban areas.	• A permanent flood barrier only closes when needed. • Barriers protect large areas of cities from the risk of very damaging flooding.	• They are very expensive. The Thames Barrier, which protects London, cost £1.6 billion to build and costs £6 million a year to maintain.
Soft engineering method	**Benefits**	**Costs**
Floodplain retention is allowing rivers to flood onto their natural floodplains. This means restricting the development of floodplains.	• Floodplain retention slows floodwaters down and reduces the risk of flooding in settlements downstream. • It is relatively cheap.	• There is an economic cost to urban areas of not building on urban floodplains. Go to page 52 to revise river flooding at Cockermouth.
River restoration involves reversing hard engineering and returning a river to its natural state. This can involve reintroducing meanders to rivers that were straightened many years ago.	• River restoration lets rivers flood along their course, reducing flooding downstream in urban areas. • Reintroducing meanders slows rivers down, reducing erosion.	• River restoration in urban areas can restrict development along river banks. • River restoration cannot prevent flooding, just reduce the risk.

 Worked example **Grades 4–6**

Figure 1 Flood wall in Hereford, UK

Study **Figure 1**, which shows a flood wall in Hereford.
Suggest **one** possible cost and **one** possible benefit of this method of flood management. **[2 marks]**

Cost: The wall might block the river view for the houses behind it.

Benefit: The extra height added means the river can rise higher without flooding the houses.

 Exam-style practice **Grades 4–6**

Explain **one** reason why soft engineering strategies are used to manage flood risk. **[2 marks]**

 Made a start **Feeling confident** 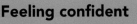 **Exam ready**

The UK's human landscape

The urban core areas and the rural areas of the UK are very different places.

 Urban core and rural areas

Urban core

Figure 1 Central London, an urban core

Population density	High: around 5500 people per km^2
Age structure	Many young adults, many single people
Economic activities	• Retail including large shops, offices, corporate headquarters, transnational corporation (TNC) headquarters • The greatest range of job opportunities
Settlement	• Conurbations, cities, large towns • Typically high-rise buildings in the centre • Property is often expensive.

Rural areas

Figure 2 A village in Somerset, a rural area

Population density	Low: under 160 people per km^2
Age structure	Many older people, some single people
Economic activities	• Farming, fishing, forestry, mining, quarrying, renewable energy, manufacturing, health, retail, working from home, tourism • Usually a small range of job opportunities
Settlement	• Market towns, villages, hamlets, isolated dwellings, farmhouses • Low-rise buildings • Property is generally cheaper than in cities.

Figure 3 A population pyramid for London in 2011

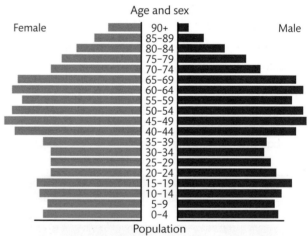

Figure 4 A population pyramid for Somerset in 2013

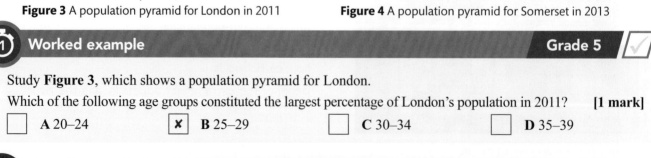

① **Worked example** — Grade 5

Study **Figure 3**, which shows a population pyramid for London.
Which of the following age groups constituted the largest percentage of London's population in 2011? **[1 mark]**

☐ **A** 20–24　　☒ **B** 25–29　　☐ **C** 30–34　　☐ **D** 35–39

② **Exam-style practice** — Grades 4–6

Figure 3 and **Figure 4** show population pyramids for an urban core (London) and a rural area (Somerset).
Describe **two** differences between **Figure 3** and **Figure 4**. **[4 marks]**

 Made a start　　 **Feeling confident**　　 **Exam ready**

Reducing differences

UK and EU government policies have attempted to reduce the differences between the urban core and rural areas through investment in transport infrastructure, regional development and the creation of enterprise zones.

(10) Investment in transport infrastructure

Port improvements
Liverpool2 is a £400 million investment to create a new deep-water terminal at the port of Liverpool in the north-west of England. This has generated new employment and boosted the local economy, helping to reduce the unemployment rate, which is higher in the north of the UK than in the south.

Smart motorways
Smart motorways, for example the M42 in the West Midlands, use technology to manage traffic actively. A control centre remotely monitors traffic and activates signs to alert drivers to hazards or changes and to close lanes. Smart motorways have been proven to reduce traffic congestion and improve journey times, but there are concerns about how safe they are.

Railway improvements
Several rail improvements schemes are being introduced, which will decrease the time it takes to travel around the UK. For example, High Speed 2 (HS2) is a plan to provide a high-speed link between the north and the south. The aim is to improve transport connections between key cities (London, Birmingham, Leeds, Manchester, Liverpool, Sheffield, Edinburgh and Glasgow) to promote economic growth.

(10) Regional development strategies

The Northern Powerhouse
This is a UK government strategy to improve quality of life and economic opportunities in rural and urban areas in the north of England and Wales. The Northern Powerhouse project has three main aspects:

1. Increased investment across the north, including investment in improving schools and tourist attractions such as national parks, cultural events and sporting events.
2. Devolution of political decisions from London, to increase the power of local people.
3. Investment in transport infrastructure to improve connectivity between rural and urban areas across the north, making it a better place to live.

Enterprise Zones
The UK government created Enterprise Zones in 2012, such as the Bristol Temple Quarter and Tees Valley Enterprise Zones. These areas offer tax breaks and superfast broadband to encourage businesses to locate there. They are helping to resolve regional differences by attracting investment to these areas and have created around 24 000 jobs.

EU policies
EU policies such as the European Regional Development Fund have provided money to local projects with the aim of reducing economic inequalities between regions.

(5) Key facts

- ☑ 15 million people live in the north; with more than 20 universities and 25 per cent of UK manufacturing located there.
- ☑ 17 enterprise zones are being created.
- ☑ £400 million of investment in smaller local businesses.

(5) Worked example   Grades 4–6

Explain **one** reason why improving transport links could help reduce differences between UK urban core areas and rural areas. **[2 marks]**

Better transport links mean that people can live in rural areas and still commute into urban areas. This helps rural areas because it means young people will not have to leave them to find a range of good jobs.

(5) Exam-style practice   Grades 4–5

Suggest **two** reasons for improvements to rail networks in the UK. **[4 marks]**

Migration and the UK

Over the last 50 years, migration has changed the population geography of the UK. Immigration policies have helped make the UK more diverse.

⑩ Population changes

Figure 1 shows changes in the UK's population structure between 2001 and 2011. This data is obtained from government censuses. You can view census data online. It can be used to understand population and demographic change.

These were the main changes between 2001 and 2011:

1 The number of children under 5 increased.

2 The number of 20–25 year olds increased.

3 More people lived to over 80.

International migration is one important reason for these changes, because:

- migrants tend to be young adults, which helps explain the increase in the number of 20–25 year olds
- young adults start families, which helps explain the increase in the number of babies and young children
- health services employ migrants to care for the UK's ageing population and care helps people to live longer.

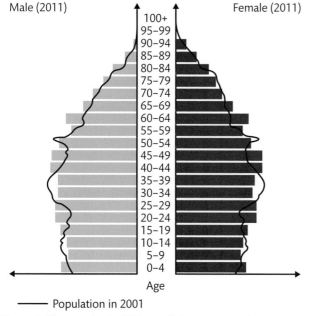

Male (2011)   Female (2011)

— Population in 2001

Figure 1 Changes in the UK population structure between 2001 and 2011

⑤ Worked example   Grades 4–6

Using **Figure 1**, suggest **one** reason for the changes to the UK's population structure from 2001 to 2011. **[2 marks]**

Figure 1 shows that there has been an increase of people between 30 and 44 years of age since 2001. This could be the result of young migrants coming into the UK from the EU looking for employment.

⑤ Internal migration

Many places within the UK have experienced population changes as groups of people move from one area to another:

- Some of the UK's biggest cities, such as London, Manchester and Birmingham, have seen an increase in young people moving into the city, for the many job opportunities and universities. The population of these places has therefore become more youthful.
- Many older people, have moved out of urban areas into more scenic and peaceful rural areas, such as the south coast and south-west to enjoy their retirement.

⑤ Migration to the UK

Before June 2016, immigration to the UK from the European Union (EU) was increasing. People from EU countries have the right to live and work in other EU countries under the EU's Citizens' Rights Directive of 2004. The number of people moving to other EU countries increased after the enlargement of the EU in 2004, to include eight Eastern and Central European countries, including Poland, and also in 2007 when Bulgaria and Romania joined the EU. In June 2016, the UK voted to leave the EU (Brexit). Many British people wanted to reduce the number of immigrants to the UK.

Migration statistics

- In 2016, 9.2 million people living in the UK had not been born there.
- 3.5 million of those people were born in EU countries, and of those about 1 million were born in Poland.
- Of those from outside the EU, 830 000 were from India and 520 000 from Pakistan.

Regional differences

- Most immigrants to the UK move to urban areas, where there are more job opportunities. This has contributed to UK urbanisation in the last 50 years.
- The most popular destination for migrants in the UK is London. London voted against leaving the EU.
- Northern Ireland was the only UK region with more emigrants than immigrants. Northern Ireland also voted against leaving the EU in 2016.
- The south coast of the UK is a popular area for retirement as it has warmer than average temperatures than the north.

⑤ Exam-style practice   Grades 4–6

Every year, nearly 3 million UK citizens migrate from one part of the UK to another. Suggest **two** reasons why people migrate within the UK. **[4 marks]**

Economic change in the UK

Primary and secondary industries have declined across the UK in recent years, affecting both urban and rural areas differently. You need to know how contrasting regions of the UK have been affected by this economic change.

 ## The decline in primary industry

Many rural areas have been affected by the decline of primary industries, such as mining and farming, whilst many urban areas have been affected by the decline in secondary industries, such as manufacturing.

For example, the rural communities of South Wales have been affected by the decline of the coal mining industry. Also the more urban areas of the North East, have also been affected by a decline in mining, with a knock-on effect on steel production and ship building.

All of the coal that was easily accessible in the UK's pits has now been mined and it is cheaper for the UK to import coal from the USA and Australia. As a result, all of the coal mines in the UK have closed, resulting in high levels of unemployment in the local areas. Many people relied on the work from the coal industry and other associated industries. Unemployment in rural areas of the UK, such as Scotland, and urban areas that have traditionally relied on manufacturing, such as the North East and the Midlands, is higher than the UK average of 3.8 per cent. In 2019, Scotland had an unemployment rate of 4 per cent and the North East had an unemployment rate of 5 per cent.

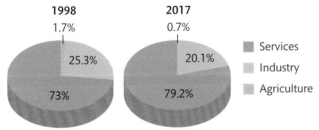

Figure 1 Changes in economic structure in the UK between 1998 and 2017.

Other reasons might include: that the UK has increasingly imported food and other primary products from abroad resulting in a decline in primary industries, and/or as the UK's population has become more educated, more people work in highly skilled tertiary/quaternary professions, such as banking and law.

 ## The rise of tertiary and quaternary industries

Large urban areas, such as London and Manchester, have experienced economic growth, particularly in tertiary and quaternary industries, also known as knowledge-based industries (KBI), such as financial services, IT, law and creative industries (e.g. web design) based in areas such as Canary Wharf in London.

There are a number of reasons for the growth of knowledge-based industries in urban areas:

- **Skills and training:** Urban areas are home to large universities which provide a highly skilled UK workforce but they also attract employees from abroad.
- **Location and connectivity:** Urban areas are well connected with good access to other places and businesses, both within the UK and internationally.
- **Investment:** Both governments and FDI have invested in urban areas.

With the growth in working from home, these industries are no longer restricted to expensive urban locations.

 ## Worked example   Grades 5–6

Study **Figure 1**, which shows changes in the UK's economic structure between 1998 and 2017. Describe how the UK economy has changed since 1998.   **[2 marks]**

The agriculture and industry sectors in the UK have decreased since 1998. Agriculture has decreased by 1% and industry by 5%, while the service sector has increased by 6.2%.

Suggest **one** reason why the UK economy has changed since 1998.   **[2 marks]**

Many manufacturing industries have moved to developing or emerging countries like China, where the goods can be produced cheaper. This has resulted in a decline in manufacturing industry, known as deindustrialisation, in the UK.

 ## Exam-style practice   Grades 5–6

Explain why some urban areas have experienced economic growth in recent years.   **[4 marks]**

Investing in the UK

When other countries invest in the UK, this is called foreign direct investment (FDI). Globalisation, free trade policies and privatisation have increased the amount of FDI in the UK.

FDI in the UK

Foreign direct investment in the UK increases and decreases over the years.

There are three main reasons why FDI increases:

1. **Globalisation** is the increasing number of connections between countries. It is based on money moving almost instantly around the world. London is a global centre for banking and financial services.

2. **Free trade** policies have encouraged FDI. The UK has been part of the European Union (EU). The EU encourages free trade and makes investment between its member countries easy.

3. **Privatisation** by UK governments has encouraged FDI. The government has privatised companies and encouraged foreign investors to buy them. For example, ScottishPower is owned by a Spanish company called Iberdrola.

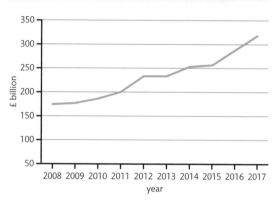

Figure 1 Inward FDI from foreign companies in the UK from 2008 to 2017

The role of TNCs

Transnational corporations (TNCs) encourage FDI because they buy and sell companies in different countries all over the world. TNCs have invested in the UK economy. This has advantages and disadvantages for the UK.

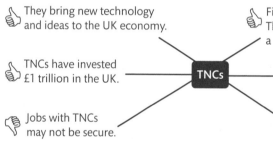

They bring new technology and ideas to the UK economy.

TNCs have invested £1 trillion in the UK.

Jobs with TNCs may not be secure.

Financial services TNCs locate in London. The UK economy receives over £200 billion a year from financial services.

London has benefitted from TNCs more than anywhere else in the UK.

TNCs can outcompete British companies, forcing them to close.

Worked example Grades 4–6

Figure 2 Steelworks in South Wales

Study **Figure 2**, which shows a steelworks in South Wales that is owned by an Indian company. Explain **one** advantage and **one** disadvantage of working for this TNC. **[4 marks]**

One advantage is that a TNC could export the steel to lots of different markets all over the world, helping the company to grow. One disadvantage might be that jobs at the steelworks are less secure, because the TNC might cut jobs in Britain rather than in India if it needed to save money.

Investors in the UK

The three countries that invested the most in Britain in 2013 were:

1. the USA (47 per cent of all FDI)
2. Canada (9 per cent)
3. Spain (5 per cent).

In the same year, the top three sectors of the economy that FDI went into were:

1. financial services (46 per cent of all FDI)
2. information and communication (19 per cent)
3. transport and logistics (planning how to produce and transport things) (8 per cent).

Exam-style practice Grades 3–5

Explain **two** reasons why foreign direct investment (FDI) might increase in the UK. **[4 marks]**

 Made a start   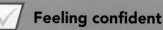 **Feeling confident**   **Exam ready**

A major UK city: London

You need to know about a case study of a dynamic UK city. This is a case study on London. You should revise the case study you studied in class

⑤ Case study

The location and importance of London

- **Site:** London is the UK's largest city, located in the south-east of the UK. The site was chosen by the Romans as a crossing point of the River Thames.
- **Situation:** London was a large port for trading by sea. The city grew outwards from the River Thames and now has the M25 orbital motorway around its outer parts. It is in a central global location, both physically and in terms of time zone, making it ideal for regular business travellers.
- **Connectivity:** London is a global hub. It is connected to other major cities of the UK through an extensive motorway and train network. Heathrow and Gatwick airports connect London to most of the world's major cities.

② Cultural diversity

International migration has made London one of the most culturally diverse cities in the UK. Migrants have introduced different types of foods, entertainment and clothing. For example, Brick Lane is a vibrant mix of multicultural cafes, restaurants, markets and shops. London continues to attract migrants to work in its knowledge-based industries.

Figure 1 Festival in Brick Lane, London

⑩ London's structure

Cities are composed of different areas:

Central Business District (CBD)

- This is the heart of the city, which is dominated by large high-density shops, offices, theatres and hotels.
- London has two CBD – the West End and Canary Wharf.

Inner City

- These areas were once home to industry and high-density housing.
- As many of the factories have closed and people have left for the suburbs, these areas became derelict and run-down and the environment left in a poor state.
- Many inner-city areas in London (e.g. Hackney and Docklands) have been redeveloped. Warehouses have now become modern apartments with surrounding parks and leisure facilities.

Suburbs

- These can be found beyond the inner city towards the edges of cities.
- In the outer suburbs, low density housing can be found and the quality of the environment is high.
- The inner suburbs vary from expensive areas (e.g. Kensington and Chelsea) to areas of old factories and new apartments (e.g. Hackney). The inner suburbs were built in the 19th century (1920s and 30s), with the outer suburbs (e.g. Wembley) built in the 1950s and 1960s.

Urban-rural fringe

- This is the area of countryside next to and closely linked to the city (e.g. St Albans).
- It is mainly residential, with low-density housing (most houses have a garden) and higher environmental quality.

② Worked example   Grades 2–3

State **two** features of the urban-rural fringe   **[2 marks]**

There are lots of green open spaces. The buildings are low rise.

⑤ Exam-style practice   Grades 5–6

For a named UK city, explain why the environmental quality varies in the different parts of the city.   **[3 marks]**

Population changes

Dynamic cities are affected by migration. People are attracted to cities because of the opportunities they offer. This case study is about London.

(5) Migration in London

- London is very attractive to migrants from other parts of the UK and abroad because it has well-paid jobs and many opportunities.
- More people born outside the UK live in London than anywhere else in the UK.
- Migrants often settle in the inner city for several reasons. Economic reasons include the fact that rents here are cheaper than elsewhere in the city, because housing quality is lower. Social reasons include the fact that the inner city often houses communities of people from migrants' home countries, making it very ethnically diverse.
- International migrants make London one of the most culturally diverse cities in the UK. Migrants have introduced different types of foods, entertainment and clothing.

(5) Reasons for migration

National – The pull factor for many young people from within the UK to cities, such as London, is good universities, with more well-paid skilled job opportunities and a city lifestyle, with more entertainment.

International – many migrants from the EU and other countries (such as Australia and the USA) come to the UK and London for employment. Migrants from other countries, such as India and other Asian countries, come to join family already settled in the UK. Some migrants are refugees escaping persecution or conflict.

(5) The impact of migration on London

	London borough	
	Kensington & Chelsea	**Tower Hamlets**
Age structure	More elderly people – 14.3% over 65	Fewer elderly people – 6% over 65
	Fewer working-age people (16–64) – 69.3%	More working-age people (16–64) – 73.9%
Ethnicity and culture	65% white, 12% Asian, 9% African/Caribbean	46% white, 41% Asian, 7% African/Caribbean
	Largely white middle-class population	Largest Bangladeshi community in the UK – 33% of the population.
Housing	More people own their home (37.7 %)	More rented property (73.1 %)

(10) Exam-style practice Grades 4–6

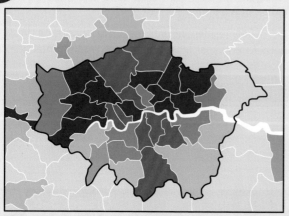

Figure 1 Ethnic population of London

1 Study **Figure 1**, which shows the ethnic population across London. Describe the distribution of London's ethnic population. **[3 marks]**

2 Suggest **two** reasons for the distribution. **[4 marks]**

Greater London

Ethnic* population as % of total, 2011

>60.0	50.0–60.0	40.0–49.9	30.0–39.9	20.0–29.9	<20.0

*Excludes British whites and Irish

 Made a start   **Feeling confident**   **Exam ready**

Unequal London

You need to know about reasons for inequality and areas of decline in your case study city. This case study is about London.

Inequality in London

Although some parts of London are very wealthy, others are poor: this is **inequality**. However, inequality does not only refer to wealth. In more deprived areas there may be:

- higher unemployment and more people living on low incomes
- more health problems and lower life expectancies
- fewer services, as organisations are less likely to invest there and people do not have a large disposable income
- a higher percentage of young people leaving education without qualifications.

The Index of Multiple Deprivation (IMD) combines different measures of deprivation, such as wage levels, education and qualifications, crime levels, and living environment. **Figure 1** shows IMD data for part of London.

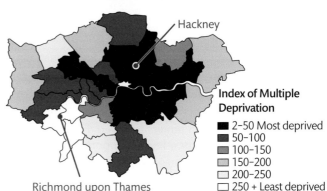

Index of Multiple Deprivation
- 2–50 Most deprived
- 50–100
- 100–150
- 150–200
- 200–250
- 250 + Least deprived

Figure 1 Index of Multiple Deprivation for London.

Indicators of inequality

	Hackney	Richmond upon Thames
Employment: Unemployment (%)	11	3
Health and disability: Childhood obesity (%)	27	13
Education, skills and training:		
GCSE students (attaining 5 GCSEs inc Maths and English)(%)	60	63
Children entitled to free school meals (%)	40	14
People working in managerial, professional and technical professions (%)	57	72

Figure 2 Indicators of employment, health and education for two London Boroughs

Decline in London

Three reasons why parts of London have experienced decline are:

- **Deindustrialisation**: Deprived areas are often areas that used to have industries, but do not any more. In the 1930s, around 100 000 people worked in London's docks and there were many manufacturing industries. Global economic changes meant the docks closed and manufacturing moved out of the city.

- **Depopulation**: as industries left London, people left, too. Depopulated areas became run-down, meaning more people left them, which increased depopulation.

- **Decentralisation**: London's centre was very congested. Businesses moved out to the rural–urban fringe, where people could drive to them more easily and rents were lower. Deprived areas in the inner city were left behind. E-commerce (online shopping) has also contributed to economic decline.

Worked example — Grades 3–5

Study **Figure 1** which shows the Index of Multiple Deprivation for London. Describe the pattern of deprivation across London Boroughs. **[2 marks]**

The most deprived areas are in the central areas of London, towards the north and east. The outer parts of the city have the areas of least deprivation.

Exam-style practice — Grades 4–6

Study **Figures 1 and 2**. Suggest why there are variations in quality of life in London. **[4 marks]**

 Made a start 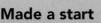 **Feeling confident** **Exam ready**

Growth and regeneration

You need to know about reasons for, and impacts of, growth and regeneration in your case study city. This case study is about London.

 Growth in London

While some areas have experienced decline, other parts of London have grown.

- London has grown outwards (**urban sprawl**) due to development on its rural–urban fringe.
- Redevelopment of London's dockland areas created a new financial centre. Spectacular growth in financial services involved transnational corporations (TNCs) investing in new headquarters in the City of London.
- **Gentrification** of parts of London's inner city followed, as wealthier people wanted to live closer to their jobs. Gentrification is renovation of older buildings and improvement of local services as wealthier people move to an area.
- A major regeneration project followed the 2012 Olympic Games. The site of the Games, now the Queen Elizabeth Olympic Park, offers new **leisure** opportunities. There are also plans for over 10 000 new homes to be built.
- London's universities are very popular with students from around the world. This has led to **studentification** of some areas.

 Regeneration and rebranding

- **Regeneration** is redeveloping an urban area to make it more attractive. For example, London's deindustrialised Lea Valley was regenerated into the Olympic Park.
- **Rebranding** is about changing the image of an urban area. For example, Stratford in East London has been rebranded as an exciting place to go shopping, following its regeneration.

	Positive impacts	Negative impacts
Increased population	• Becomes a more popular place to live. • More shops and services open.	• House prices and rents increase. • Area is less affordable for original population.
Environmental quality	• Contaminated land is cleaned up. • Pollution to rivers is cleaned up. • Housing redeveloped so it is clean, safe and attractive.	• Reduces available green space. • Land is more profitable for house building so more homes are packed in.
Economic opportunities	• Attracts new businesses, creates jobs and economic growth. • Increased taxes from growth can be spent on further regeneration.	• Foreign investment in London property has increased prices. • Some areas unaffordable to British people.

 Worked example Grades 4–5

Study **Figure 1**, which shows an OS map extract of Stratford in East London. The area was further regenerated for the 2012 Olympics.

Suggest **two** ways in which regeneration has improved the quality of life for the people in this area. **[2 marks]**

The university will help people to gain the skills needed for higher paying jobs. The stadium will provide jobs and boost the economy.

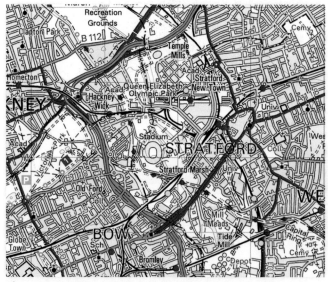

Figure 1 An OS map extract of Stratford in East London. The scale is 1:50 000.

 Exam-style practice Grades 5–6

For a named UK city, explain **one** advantage and **one** disadvantage of regeneration. **[4 marks]**

Sustainable London

You need to know about strategies aimed at making urban life more sustainable in your case study city.

 (10) Sustainable urban living

Ways to improve quality of life and sustainability in urban areas include:

Recycling
Urban areas produce a huge amount of waste. Currently, London only recycles 32 per cent of its rubbish – the UK average is 43 per cent. Improving recycling would make urban life more sustainable. Waste can also be burnt to generate electricity.

Transport
Congestion creates air pollution, releases greenhouse gases and costs businesses time and money. Encouraging people to use public transport in urban areas is more sustainable. London enforces congestion charges for using cars and uses the money to improve public transport. It also introduced a bike rental scheme.

Housing
Gentrification of areas (e.g. Hackney) that were previously run down has helped to improve the quality of the environment.
Energy-efficient new homes with good insulation require less energy to keep warm, improving their sustainability.

Affordable housing schemes and shared ownership schemes in the city make at least some housing in new developments cheaper, which contributes to sustainability by reducing the number of people who commute long distances.

Employment
Many businesses/places of employment are working to reduce their carbon footprint by recycling, going paperless and using electronic communications. More London, a development of office buildings, shops and restaurants on the south bank of the Thames, has solar panels for hot water, green roofs to support wildlife and is fuelled by recycled biodiesel from waste cooking oil from local restaurants.

Green spaces
Green spaces provide much-needed areas for leisure and relaxation, which improve quality of life. London has over 3000 parks and green spaces. Victoria Park, part of the Olympic Park, was created as part of the redevelopment of the area for 2012 Olympics. However, the pressure for housing may restrict the amount of green space.

 (5) Worked example Grades 4–6

Figure 1 Hyde Park in London

Study **Figure 1**, which shows a park in central London. Explain the impacts of green spaces on quality of life in urban areas. **[4 marks]**

Green spaces provide places for people to relax and enjoy leisure pursuits, improving their quality of life. Vegetation helps to remove air pollution and CO_2, reducing urban greenhouse gas emissions.

Green spaces may also have negative impacts on quality of life. They may become areas that are difficult to police, where people are mugged or take drugs. They also occupy land that could otherwise be used for affordable housing. As a result, people may not be able to find somewhere affordable to live in the city, so they may have to commute long distances, which is bad for quality of life.

 (5) Exam-style practice Grades 4–6

For a named UK city, explain how transport can be made more sustainable. **[4 marks]**

 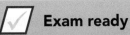

Challenges facing rural areas

The city and the accessible rural areas around it are interdependent. You need to know about challenges and opportunities in rural areas linked to your case study city.

(15) Accessible rural areas

Accessible rural areas are easy to get to from urban areas. They may be close enough for people to live in them and commute to the city. A city and its accessible rural areas are interdependent, and there are flows of goods, money and people between them. This creates opportunities and challenges in the rural area.

👍 **Counter-urbanisation** brings people and money to rural areas. Local shops gain customers, local schools get more students, local house prices increase and there is demand for leisure services such as golf courses. These are all economic and social benefits for accessible rural areas.

👎 People moving to rural areas and commuting to work brings a social benefit for the city by reducing pressure on housing. However, people who move from the city to rural areas have higher salaries than local residents, which can bring an economic cost by making house prices rise above the level that local people can afford.

👍 An increased population in accessible rural areas creates a demand for leisure and recreation, which can create opportunities for diversification. These may include opening farm shops, creating tourism projects, and catering for new leisure activities. These bring economic benefits to the rural area.

👎 **Rural diversification** involves development of the countryside. Farmland and woodland may be developed for housing or leisure services such as golf courses. This has environmental impacts, as wildlife habitats are lost, and it can contribute to the decline in primary employment in jobs such as farming.

👍 Life in rural areas can pose challenges to particular groups. For example, elderly people may have difficulty accessing healthcare and there may be limited job opportunities for younger people. Changes to rural areas can create economic and social benefits including access to hospitals in the city and job opportunities other than farming.

(5) Worked example   Grades 4–6

Study **Figure 1**, which shows an annotated aerial photo of an accessible rural area south-east of London. Mornshill Farm is located on the right of the photo.

Suggest **two** ways in which Mornshill Farm could diversify to create new economic opportunities.

[4 marks]

Figure 1 An annotated aerial photo of Effingham, an accessible rural area near London.

People from the city might want to buy farm products from Mornshill Farm, so it could open a farm shop and sell its produce to generate additional income. It could advertise its shop at Effingham Junction railway station as lots of people probably commute into the city from there every day.

Mornshill Farm could also run leisure activities. There is already a golf course in Effingham but the farm could run activities such as clay pigeon shooting or quad biking in the evenings and weekends to earn extra money.

(2) Exam-style practice   Grades 3–5

Developers want to relocate the local school (in **Figure 1**) to Effingham Common (in the south of the photo) and build expensive flats on the school's old site.

Suggest **one** environmental impact of using Effingham Common for development.   **[2 marks]**

✓ **Made a start**   ✓ **Feeling confident**   ✓ **Exam ready**

Human geography enquiries

You are required to carry out **two** contrasting geographical investigations.

 Investigating the human environment

You should have carried out fieldwork in either an urban or rural area to investigate how and why quality of life varies within that urban area or how and why deprivation occurs within rural areas. You will be asked questions on the fieldwork you did and also to apply your fieldwork skills to an unfamiliar human fieldwork scenario.

 The Enquiry process

For each stage in this process you need to be able to explain what you did and why you did it, and evaluate the advantages and disadvantages of the process.

Six stage enquiries

1 **Identify suitable enquiry questions** – can your enquiry be investigated through fieldwork?

2 **Collecting data** – decide on appropriate methods for collecting primary and secondary data; identify any risks and plan risk mitigation.

3 **Select appropriate methods of processing and presenting data** – select appropriate methods and explain your reasons for using these methods.

4 **Analysing and explaining your data** – use appropriate statistical techniques and explain any anomalies. Can geographical theories be used to help explain your results?

5 **Reaching conclusions** – draw evidenced conclusions related to the original aim and hypothesis of your enquiry.

6 **Reflecting critically** – identify the advantages and limitations of your data collection, your data, the reliability of your conclusions and your learning throughout the fieldwork process.

You also need to be able to apply this process to questions on 'unfamiliar' fieldwork scenarios.

Formulating enquiry questions

- You need to know what kinds of enquiry questions can be investigated through human fieldwork and the geographical theory or concepts that underpin your fieldwork.
- You need to be able devise suitable enquiry questions that can be tested through fieldwork.
- You may be asked to explain the ones you used for your human fieldwork or to devise enquiry questions around resources given in the exam.

Justifying the choice of location and selecting sites

You will need to explain your choice of the location you used to conduct your investigation and the suitability of the sites selected. You will need to make sure that the sites used are different enough to show a contrast, and that they are accessible and safe areas in which to conduct fieldwork.

Figure 1 Two different urban areas of Salford

 Worked example **Grades 3–5**

Study **Figure 1**, which are photographs of two areas 3 km apart in an inner-city area of Salford chosen by a group of students studying how and why quality of life varies within an urban area.

The students chose to do an environmental quality survey at each site and to conduct questionnaires on a Thursday afternoon to get the views of the people living in this area.

Suggest a suitable enquiry question or hypothesis that students might have proposed for their investigation. **[2 marks]**

1. Why does the quality of the environment vary between location A and B?

2. People in location B will have a better quality of life than those in location A.

Exam-style practice **Grades 4–6**

Suggest **two** problems that the students' choice of location may have caused for data collection. **[4 marks]**

Human geography data collection

You need to understand how to collect, measure and record fieldwork data for human geography enquiries. You'll need to use several different methods of data collection and be able to justify your methods.

(5) Key terms

- **Quantitative data** is numerical or fact-based. An example of a quantitative method would be counting the number of pedestrians walking past a particular point.
- **Qualitative data** is non-numerical and opinion-based. An example of a qualitative method would be a questionnaire.
- **Primary data** is data that you collect yourself in the field. This might be done individually, in pairs or in small groups.
- **Secondary data** is data that has been obtained from another person or organisation, such as the Environment Agency or the Office for National Statistics. This type of data is important in generating background information for the study, which can help to support your own primary data.

(2) Geographical skills

Each type of data has advantages and disadvantages. For example:

Quantitative data
- 👍 More easily analysed and presented (e.g. graphical formats).
- 👍 Easy to identify trends/patterns.
- 👍 Can be compared with other data.
- 👎 May lack reliability if sample size is not representative.
- 👎 Doesn't explain reasons for patterns/trends.

Qualitative data
- 👍 Gives more insight/opinions.
- 👍 Explains reasons for patterns/trends.
- 👎 More difficult to compare, analyse and draw conclusions.
- 👎 Based around opinions, which may introduce bias.

You need to know which type of data is best suited to your chosen enquiry. You could use more than one type of data in your enquiry.

(2) Exam focus

You should have used one quantitative fieldwork method to collect data on environmental quality. This could have been an environmental quality survey, a traffic count, a litter count or a count of the trees in an area.

You should have used one qualitative fieldwork method to collect views and perceptions on quality of life or deprivation. This could have involved drawing a field sketch or annotating photos of the place/main features you observed, or conducting a questionnaire to find out peoples' views or opinions.

Figure 1 Students conducting a questionnaire by asking opinions to generate qualitative data

(2) Worked example — Grades 4–6

Study **Figure 1**. Explain **one** disadvantage of using the technique shown. **[2 marks]**

Figure 1 shows a student conducting a questionnaire. One problem with questionnaires is that they can be subjective according to the person and group of people asked. Young people's views about an urban environment will be very different to those of older people.

(5) Exam-style practice — Grades 4–6

You have carried out your own fieldwork investigating why quality of life varies within an urban environment or why deprivation varies within a rural environment. Explain **one** advantage of a quantitative fieldwork method you used in your investigation. **[2 marks]**

 Made a start   **Feeling confident**   **Exam ready**

Presenting human geography data

You need to know how to choose suitable presentation techniques to represent the data you have collected in your geographical investigations and how to interpret and analyse data presented in different ways.

 ## (15) Types of data presentation

Human geography data can be presented in several ways. For example, land-use maps, divided bar charts, flow-line maps, choropleth maps and/or annotated photographs and/or field sketches.

It is important that you can justify your choice of data presentation and discuss the advantages and disadvantages of the techniques you used.

Technique	Use	Advantages	Disadvantages
Pie Charts	Useful for showing the % values of statistical data	Good visual presentation of data. Simple and easy to construct and understand	Too many categories make the charts cluttered and difficult to read. Reading absolute values from the graphs can be difficult.
Sketch maps	Useful to show a rough map of a study area	Quick and easy to show a map of an area.	May not be an accurate representation of a place.
Radar graphs	Useful to show multiple factors	Several independent variables can be represented.	Only a limited data range can be presented.

Remember you may be asked to explain the advantages and disadvantages of unfamiliar data presentation techniques

 ## (2) Exam focus

Annotated diagrams

You may be asked to show how you presented your data as an annotated sketch (e.g. an annotated land-use map). This should not be a work of art and nor take too much time. However, you need to make sure your diagram is clear and not too cluttered, with the key features labelled and clearly annotated with detailed but brief description. You need to remember to include a scale and direction arrow. For example:

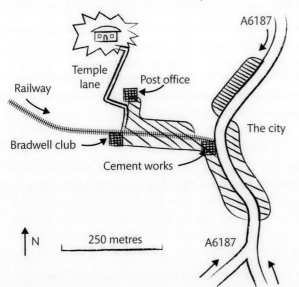

Figure 2 A sketch map

 ## (2) Worked example Grades 3–5

Figure 1 A word cloud showing perceptions of a rural area

Study **Figure 1**, which shows the results of an investigation carried out by GCSE students into perceptions of a rural area. Describe the results presented in **Figure 1**. **[2 marks]**

The area is described as mainly quiet, peaceful and tranquil, but also boring.

 ## (5) Exam-style practice Grades 4–6

Using an annotated diagram that you used to present the results of your data collection, explain your results. **[4 marks]**

 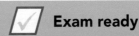

Physical geography enquiries

You are required to carry out **two** contrasting geographical investigations.

② Investigating the physical environment

You should have carried out fieldwork on either a coast or river to investigate the impact of coastal management on coastal processes and communities, or how and why drainage basin characteristics influence flood risk to people and property. You will be asked questions on the fieldwork you did and also to apply your fieldwork skills to an unfamiliar physical fieldwork scenario.

② The enquiry process

For each stage in this process (see page 65), you need to be able to explain what you did and why you did it, and evaluate the advantages and disadvantages of the process.

① Exam focus

When devising physical enquiry questions, refer back to the theory and concepts you have studied on that topic. Use maps and photos of the area you are investigating to help you devise fieldwork questions that you could investigate.

② Choosing your questions and sites

Make sure your questions can be tested and that they are suitable for the area you are visiting, and for the time and equipment you have available.

You will need to make sure that the sites you have selected are accessible and safe areas in which to conduct fieldwork.

⑩ Worked example   Grades 7–9

Figure 1 An OS map extract showing the River Ise and its catchment. The scale is 1:50 000.

> You need to refer to the geographical theory you have studied and make a judgement about whether your suggested enquiry questions could be tested in this area.

> Using your geographical skills, take specific information from the map. Be specific about places and features.

Study **Figure 1**. A group of GCSE Geography students have decided that this would be a good area to investigate how and why drainage basin characteristics influence flood risk for people and property. Assess the different enquiry questions about this environment that they might investigate.   **[8 marks]**

Students could investigate whether river discharge increases with distance downstream (Bradshaw model). They could measure the river's width, depth and discharge at two sites to test this. They could select a site in the north of the area (e.g. Newton), where the river is accessible by a footpath from the road near the pub in Geddington. They could compare this with a site further south, where the river flows close to the settlement of Warkton. Again, the river is accessible by footpath. However, the river in this area may not have enough contrast as it appears quite uniform.

Another enquiry that students could investigate would be whether the land use adjacent to the river affects the risk of flooding. This is a suitable enquiry question as the river flows through different contrasting land uses. In the north of the area, the river flows through woodland, which might mean there is less risk of flooding as the trees intercept and absorb water, reducing the river's discharge.

As the river flows through the settlement where there is a ford it passes under the road. There will be more tarmac and other impermeable surfaces so the water will run off into the river more quickly, increasing the discharge and the risk of flooding. Further information would be useful about the area such as the geology and climate data.

> Think about any issues and problems the area might have and what other information you might need.

⑤ Exam-style practice   Grades 3–5

You have carried out your own fieldwork investigation in a physical environment. For your named environment, state an enquiry question you devised and explain how theories or concepts helped you devise your enquiry question.   **[2 marks]**

 Made a start   **Feeling confident**   **Exam ready**

Physical geography data collection

You need to understand how to collect, measure and record fieldwork data for physical geography enquiries. You'll need to use several different methods of data collection and be able to justify your methods.

Sampling methods

For each method, it is important that you decide where and how you will collect the data. It is not possible or practical for you to collect every relevant piece of data, so a representative sample should be taken. There are three types of sampling:

1 **Random sampling** – collecting data at random, for example picking up stones from any part of a river bed.

2 **Systematic sampling** – collecting data at specific intervals, for example measuring the depth of the river at 30 cm intervals.

3 **Stratified sampling** – collecting data from different subsets of a parent population in order to obtain a fair representation of each group. The subsets have a known size. An example is collecting information from different age groups during a survey. Stratified sampling can be either random or systematic.

> Refer back to the key terms on page 66 to remind yourself of the different types of data that can be collected.

It is important to know the advantages and disadvantages of the sampling techniques that you have used.

Exam focus
For example,
Random sampling
👍 Each member of the population has an equal chance of being included.
👎 May not represent the wider area/population if sample points are clustered in one area.
Systematic sampling
👍 More straightforward to do.
👍 Gives good coverage of study area at regular intervals.
Stratified sampling
👍 Can ensure better representation of the larger area/population across the subsets.
👍 Useful when making comparisons between variables.

Worked example   Grades 6–9

A group of students studying beach profiles in two different locations collected beach sediment systematically every 25 metres along a transect, using a quadrat.

Explain **one** advantage and **one** disadvantage of this sampling technique.   **[4 marks]**

An advantage of systematic sampling is that it allows a large area of the beach to be sampled in a short period of time. It would be expected that the data collected would represent the range of sediment found along the beach.

One problem with systematic sampling is that if the interval area is large then a particular size of sediment could be missed out and therefore not represented in the collected data.

OS maps show the height and gradient of the land. The scale can be used to measure the distance between places.

Worked example   Grades 4–6

Explain how the use of Ordnance Survey (OS) maps helped you choose the location of your river OR coastal locations and sites.   **[4 marks]**

OS maps can be used to find the distance between place, which can help to plan out the fieldwork day in terms of how long it might take to travel to the fieldwork location and between the sites.

OS maps show land use and how accessible a location and site is, i.e. whether it is close to a road or footpath.

Exam-style practice   Grades 6–9

You have carried out your own fieldwork either investigating how and why drainage basin characteristics influence flood risk or the impact of coastal management on coastal processes and communities.

For your named location, assess the role of secondary data sources in your investigation.   **[8 marks]**

 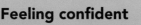

Presenting physical geography data

You need to know how to choose suitable presentation techniques to represent the data you have collected in your geographical investigations and how to interpret and analyse data presented in different ways.

(10) Types of data presentation

Depending on the study you complete, there are a range of presentation techniques that you can use. The following are suggestions of data presentation techniques that are appropriate for particular topics. You can use both hand-drawn and computer-generated methods to present information.

For rivers/coasts, you can use: cross profiles and/or scattergraphs, maps with located graphs (e.g. proportional sediment size), bar charts, annotated field sketches and/or photographs.

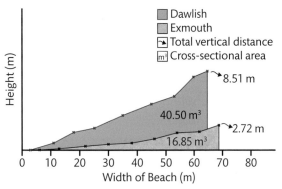

Figure 1 A beach transect showing the contrast in height of two different beaches.

Figure 2 A radar diagram for bi-polar evaluation of sea defences.

(5) Worked example   Grades 3–4

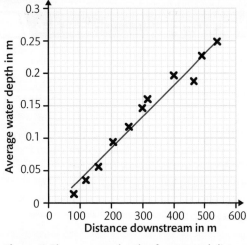

Figure 3 The average depth of water and distance downstream, Loughton Brook River

Study **Figure 3**, which shows water depth data for one area of a river.

(a) Draw a line of best fit.

[1 mark]

(b) Describe the relationship between mean average water depth and distance downstream.

[3 marks]

Figure 3 shows a strong positive correlation, which means that mean water depth increases with distance downstream. At 120 m downstream the mean water depth is 0.05 m, whereas at 540 m downstream the mean water depth is 0.25 m.

Remember, when answering questions about graphs, maps and other visual data presentation methods, you need to support your points with specific data.

(2) Exam focus

In the exam, you might be asked to justify your choice of data presentation. Go to pages 93 and 94 to revise the advantages and disadvantages of the different presentation techniques.

(5) Exam-style practice   Grades 4–5

Explain **one** advantage and **one** disadvantage of a technique you used to present your data.

[4 marks]

Analysis, conclusion and evaluation

You need to know how to write a clear and focused analysis, how to draw your findings together to form a conclusion and how to critically evaluate your fieldwork enquiries.

(5) Assessing and evaluating your findings

You need to identify the main trends and patterns and also any anomalies in your data before drawing a conclusion. You will need to go back to your enquiry questions and try to answer them with the data you have collected.

- Consider whether your data is accurate and reliable
- Reflect on the methods you used and limitations of these methods
- Consider what might have affected the accuracy and reliability of your data, and how you would improve the study if you were to do it again.

(10) Worked example — Grades 6–9

A group of students conducted a geographical investigation on the River Noe in Edale.

- They collected data at two sites, 5 km apart, on the upper course of the river.
- In the four weeks leading up to the fieldwork, the antecedent weather conditions had been very hot and dry, with no rainfall.
- They measured the width and depth of the river channel at each of the sites using a measuring tape, a metre ruler and ranging poles.
- They measured the river's velocity five times at each site, by timing a floating dog biscuit over a 10-metre stretch.
- Using the data, they calculated the mean velocity and river discharge at each site.
- They presented their data as two cross-section diagrams.

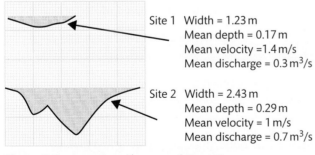

Site 1 Width = 1.23 m
Mean depth = 0.17 m
Mean velocity = 1.4 m/s
Mean discharge = 0.3 m^3/s

Site 2 Width = 2.43 m
Mean depth = 0.29 m
Mean velocity = 1 m/s
Mean discharge = 0.7 m^3/s

Figure 1 Cross section diagrams of River Noe

The students concluded that discharge increases as a river flows downstream and that flood risk is therefore greater downstream.

Assess the evidence for this conclusion.   **[8 marks]**

You need to judge how reliable and accurate you think the data is and how valid the conclusion is.

The data shows that mean discharge has increased from 0.3 m^3/s to 0.7 m^3/s as the river has flowed downstream, which supports the students' conclusion.

The river has got wider, deeper and faster from site 1 to site 2. This fits with the Bradshaw model. However, as the cross-sectional area has increased, the river has capacity to hold more water at site 2 and therefore may be less of a flood risk, which goes against the conclusion.

Site 1 is much more shallow. It would be useful to know more about the geology of this area. If the rocks around site 1 are hard and resistant to erosion, then the channel may not get eroded very easily and if there is any heavy rain the channel may flood more.

The students' data may not be entirely accurate, as they used a dog biscuit to measure velocity. This may have got stuck on obstacles in the river, which may have affected the velocity readings and discharge calculation.

The data was also collected in summer after a very dry period. The data collected may not fully represent the river channel's characteristics. If the data collected was repeated at a different time of year, then the results and conclusion may be very different.

Try to include other factors that might affect the results and conclusion.

(10) Exam-style practice — Grades 6–9

You have carried out your own fieldwork investigation in an urban or rural area.

Assess the reliability of your conclusions.   **[8 marks]**

 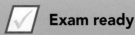

Biomes and the biosphere

The distribution of the Earth's biomes (large-scale ecosystems) is affected by climate. The biosphere is our planet's life-support system.

⑤ Distribution of major biomes

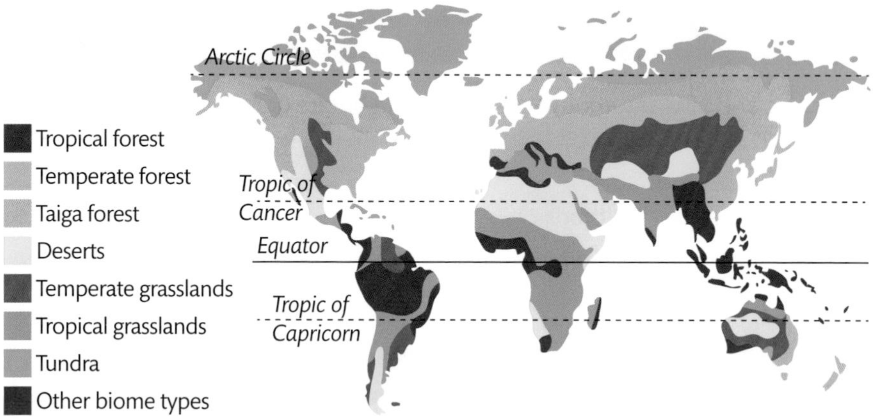

- Tropical forest
- Temperate forest
- Taiga forest
- Deserts
- Temperate grasslands
- Tropical grasslands
- Tundra
- Other biome types

Arctic Circle

Tropic of Cancer

Equator

Tropic of Capricorn

The tundra biome has low temperatures, low precipitation and few sunshine hours. The tundra biome is low in biodiversity.

Desert biomes occur in sub-tropical zones. Temperatures and sunshine are high, precipitation is low due to high pressure (see page 1: General atmospheric circulation).

Temperatures, sunshine hours and precipitation are high all year in tropical biomes, so they have very high levels of biodiversity.

Figure 1 The location of the Earth's major biomes

② Local factors

- Climate influences the distribution of biomes (where they are found) and their characteristics (what they are like).
- Biome distribution is also influenced by local factors.

Temperature decreases by 1°C for every 300 m of altitude, so mountains have different biomes to plains.

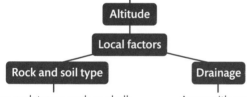

Altitude

Local factors

Rock and soil type

Some rock types, such as chalk and limestone, are permeable and let water through. Others, such as granite and clay, are impermeable.

Drainage

Areas with poor drainage, such as clay soils, become boggy.

Figure 2 Local factors affecting biome distribution

② Biome interactions

Nutrient cycles show how **biotic** (living: fauna and flora) and **abiotic** (non-living) components interact.

L = litter store
B = biomass store
S = soil store

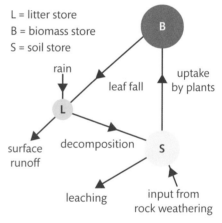

rain

leaf fall

uptake by plants

surface runoff

decomposition

leaching

input from rock weathering

Figure 3 A nutrient cycle for a tropical rainforest biome

⑤ Worked example — Grade 5

Using **Figure 1**, explain how climate affects the distribution of deserts. **[4 marks]**

The deserts are found in the sub-tropical regions of the world, where cold atmospheric air in the Hadley cell descends, warms and creates high pressure. This results in clear skies, high daytime temperatures and low annual rainfall amounts.

② Biosphere resources

The biosphere provides resources for indigenous (native) and local people, for example food such as fish, meat, berries and fruits; medicine such as morphine from poppies; building materials such as straw for roofing and timber; and fuel such as wood, dried animal dung and biofuels.

Humans exploit the biosphere and this can damage its resources. For example, mining can pollute water resources with poisonous chemicals, killing water plants, insects and fish.

⑤ Exam-style practice — Grades 5–7

Study **Figure 3**, which is a nutrient cycle for a tropical forest biome. Explain the impact on the soil store if deforestation reduces the size of the biomass store. **[2 marks]**

✓ **Made a start**   ✓ **Feeling confident**   ✓ **Exam ready**

A life-support system

The biosphere provides services that are important to all life on Earth, such as regulating our atmosphere and the water cycle, and maintaining soil health. Human activity is putting pressure on those services.

🔟 Biosphere services

The biosphere provides essential resources (food, water and energy) and three vital services.

1 It regulates the composition of the atmosphere by producing oxygen and absorbing carbon dioxide.

2 It maintains soil health by returning nutrients to soils and keeping them healthy.

3 It regulates water within the hydrological cycle, reducing flood risks and providing clean water supplies.

Figure 1 Forests are an essential part of the biosphere.

Plants take in carbon dioxide and release oxygen through photosynthesis.

Plants absorb nutrients from the soil. These nutrients are returned to the soil when leaves fall and animals and plants decompose and die.

Plants intercept rainfall, reducing surface runoff and decreasing the risk of flooding. Plant roots also encourage infiltration, increasing groundwater stores. They release water into the atmosphere through evapotranspiration, which can lead to rainfall.

🔟 Population and resources

As societies develop and population numbers grow, the demand for resources is increasing.

- The demand for food, energy, and water resources is highest in developed countries because people can afford to consume the most.
- Developing and emerging countries use less food, energy and water, but as wealth increases (rising affluence), so does the demand for resources.
- The human population is still growing rapidly, which increases the global demand for resources. The population is currenty growing at 83 million extra people a year.
- As emerging countries industrialise, their demands for water and energy increase significantly.
- The global trend towards urbanisation also increases the demand for resources.

5️⃣ Population and resource theories

Thomas Malthus' theory is that a population grows faster than food production. If a population grows too large, it will be impossible to produce enough food to feed everyone. When there are too many people to feed, famine, war or disease reduce the population again.

Ester Boserup's theory is that humans are creative under pressure and come up with innovative ways to increase food production. No matter how many people there are, we will find ways to feed them and to supply enough water and energy.

5️⃣ Worked example — Grades 4–6

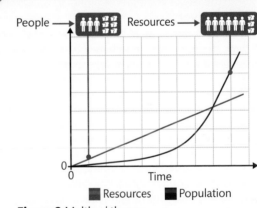

Figure 2 Malthus' theory

Study **Figure 2**, which shows Malthus' theory of population and resources. Describe the relationship between population growth and the rate by which food production can be increased.

[3 marks]

Malthus said human population increased geometrically (2, 4, 8, 16 etc.) each generation, while food production could only be increased arithmetically (1, 2, 3, 4 etc.). Therefore, Malthus' theory states that if a population grows too big, it will not be possible to feed everyone in it.

2️⃣ Exam-style practice — Grades 4–6

Suggest **one** way in which humans have been able to increase food production since Malthus' time (the 1800s).

[2 marks]

Tropical rainforest characteristics

Warm, moist tropical climates create perfect conditions for plant life, but this results in intense competition for light and nutrients.

10 Tropical rainforest adaptations ✓

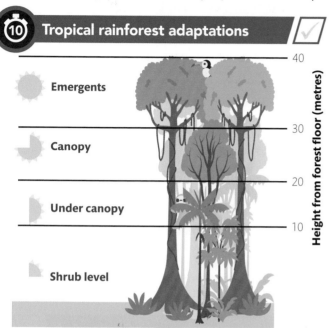

Figure 1 Tropical rainforests have stratified layers of vegetation

The emergent layer
Emergents are trees that have adapted by growing tall enough to break through the canopy. Trees here are exposed to the most sunlight of any of the layers of vegetation.

The canopy
The canopy layer is exposed to the sunlight and provides shade below. The canopy is full of birds, insects, frogs and animals such as sloths and monkeys. Animals need strong gripping hands, feet and tails to live in the high trees. When one tree falls, seedlings compete to reach the gap in the canopy by growing very rapidly. Most plants have **drip-tips** to drain water from their leaves, which stops mould building up in the wet and warm conditions.

The under canopy
More sunlight reaches the under canopy than the shrub level, but it is still shady. Plants growing here typically have very large, broad leaves to make the most of the available light. The under canopy contains woody climbing plants called lianas, which wind themselves around trees to grow up towards the sunlight.

Shrub level
Because rainforest soils only have a thin layer of nutrients near the surface, rainforest trees have shallow roots. They need **buttress roots** to keep them upright. Animals on the forest floor have adaptations for dark conditions, such as dappled camouflage. Many eat the insects that live in the litter layer on top of the soil.

5 Tropical rainforest characteristics ✓

- ✓ The climate is very wet, with over 2000 mm of rain per year.
- ✓ The climate is hot and humid all year round, with average daily temperatures of 20 °C–30 °C.
- ✓ There are perfect conditions for plant life, so there is very large **biomass**.
- ✓ There is very high **biodiversity** with complex **food webs**.
- ✓ Constant heavy rainfall leaches nutrients down through the soil, so decomposing plants and animals on the forest floor are the main source of nutrients.
- ✓ Plants compete to reach the main canopy, which blocks out light below.
- ✓ Local tribes use food and resources sustainably and live in harmony with the environment.
- ✓ Access to light creates **stratification** (layers) in the rainforest.
- ✓ Plants and animals are adapted for rainforest conditions. Animals, such as the spider monkey, have adapted to climb into the canopy where the food sources are.

5 Rapid nutrient cycling ✓

Heavy rainfall all year round

Dead plants and animals

Biomass – most of the rainforest's nutrients are stored here

Litter

Rapid decomposition in warm, wet conditions

Low surface runoff because of interception

Rapid uptake of nutrients by large biomass

Soil

Nutrients leached out of soil by rainfall

Figure 2 A tropical rainforest nutrient cycle

Tropical rainforests have a very high rate of nutrient cycling. This is because:

- Plants grow all year round, so there is a very large biomass
- Dead plants and animals decompose quickly
- The frequent heavy rainfall leaches nutrients out of the soil.

5 Exam-style practice   Grades 4–6 ✓

Study **Figure 2**, which shows a nutrient cycle for a tropical rainforest. Explain why soils in the tropical rainforest are not rich in nutrients.

[4 marks]

✓ **Made a start**   ✓ **Feeling confident**   ✓ **Exam ready**

Threats to tropical rainforest

Human activities that contribute to deforestation are direct threats to the tropical rainforest. Climate change also threatens the health of tropical rainforests.

10 Causes of deforestation

Commercial agriculture
Commercial agriculture is growing crops or rearing animals for profit. Clearing rainforest for fields to grow soybeans or to use as cattle pasture is a major cause of tropical rainforest deforestation.

Subsistence farming
Subsistence farming means people growing food to feed themselves and their families. Slash and burn techniques are often used to clear the forest. Because rainforest soils have few nutrients, soil becomes infertile quickly and new plots need to be cleared after a few years. This increases the rate of deforestation.

Mining for mineral resources
Mining methods, such as open-cast mining, clear large areas of rainforest.

Commercial hardwood logging
This contributes to deforestation because rainforest hardwood is valuable. Clear felling deforests whole areas, but even selective logging, which removes only the valuable species, opens up the rainforest for other causes of deforestation by making roads into the forest area.

Local demand for fuel wood
Rapidly rising local populations can lead to deforestation in areas where the main source of fuel is wood.

Energy production
Hydroelectric power (HEP) dams generate electricity but can involve flooding huge areas of rainforest to create reservoirs. Clearing forest to grow biofuel crops, such as palm oil, is also a major cause of deforestation.

5 Worked example — Grades 4–6

Figure 1 A false-colour satellite image of deforestation in Brazil. The light colours are deforested land, and the red is tropical rainforest.

Study **Figure 1**, which shows a satellite image of tropical rainforest deforestation.

Suggest **one** reason for the deforestation in **Figure 1**.
[2 marks]

The deforested areas are made up of small strips of cleared land, each leading out from a central road. This suggests that the reason for deforestation is subsistence agriculture, where many people have cleared a small area to grow food for their family.

5 Climate change

Workers with chainsaws cutting down trees are a direct threat to rainforests – there is a clear connection between the chainsaws and deforestation. However, not all threats are direct. Climate change is an indirect threat because it can gradually weaken the rainforest ecosystem.

Climate change is making some tropical rainforests hotter and drier. Rainforests that never had seasons before may now experience a drier season. Forests that already had drier seasons may now experience droughts.

These changes put a lot of stress on tropical rainforest ecosystems.

- Biotic and abiotic characteristics are interdependent, so many plants and animals are adapted to very specific conditions. When biotic factors such as temperature and precipitation levels change, they cannot adapt.
- Droughts mean trees die but decomposition is slow, so nutrients are released less quickly into the soil.
- When forests dry out, forest fires can occur.
- Ecosystem stress can lead to reduced biodiversity.

5 Exam-style practice — Grades 4–6

Drier conditions in tropical rainforests are reducing the amount of insect life in the litter layer. Explain **one** way in which this could affect a tropical rainforest food web.
[2 marks]

Sustainable rainforests

International laws and action by individual countries have had some successes in reducing the direct threats to tropical rainforests.

 Global actions

Two global projects that help to protect the tropical rainforest are CITES and REDD.

CITES

The Convention on International Trade in Endangered Species (CITES) lists thousands of endangered plant and animal species, bans trade in these species and requires border trade checks to make sure people do not sell the species.

👍 183 countries have signed up to CITES, so it operates on a global scale. It has succeeded in reducing the hunting of some rainforest animals, which helps to maintain biodiversity.

👎 Many developing countries cannot afford the guards needed to stop people hunting valuable animals. The convention also does not stop deforestation, which threatens biodiversity.

REDD

Reducing Emissions from Deforestation and Degradation (REDD) is an international project that funds good forest management, so that countries make more money from protecting their rainforests.

👍 REDD-funded projects protect and sustainably manage large areas of rainforest that would otherwise have been deforested.

👎 Protecting one area of the forest can mean that local people simply clear more of the unprotected areas. Local people may lose their rights to forest products without compensation.

 Sustainable forest management

A disadvantage of some global actions to protect rainforests is that they do not tackle key causes of deforestation. Growing populations of poorer people in tropical countries need land to grow food and make money to live.

Sustainable forest management involves providing alternative livelihoods for local people so that they benefit from the rainforest:

- **Ecotourism** provides local people with jobs as guides and lets local communities make money from rich tourists who come to see the rainforest.

- **Afforestation** provides local people with jobs growing and planting trees to replace those cut down by selective logging.

- **Sustainable farming** methods can maintain soil fertility and growing crops among trees can help prevent erosion and deforestation.

Sustainable management of tropical rainforests is vital for their protection. Sustainability is defined by the UN as 'development that meets the needs of the present without compromising the ability of future generations to meet their own needs'.

 Worked example — **Grades 4–6**

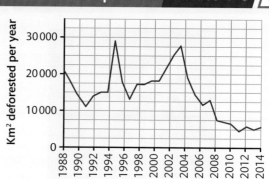

Figure 1 Deforestation in the Brazilian Amazon

Study **Figure 1**, which shows deforestation in the Amazon rainforest in Brazil, 1988–2014.

Suggest **one** reason for the trend shown in **Figure 1**.
[2 marks]

One reason could be sustainable management practices such as agroforestry or ecotourism being implemented. These let local people benefit from protecting the rainforest rather than destroying it, reducing deforestation.

 Exam-style practice — **Grades 4–6**

1. Study **Figure 1**, which shows the changing rate of deforestation in the Amazon rainforest. Suggest **one** reason for the increase in deforestation between 1996 and 2004. **[2 marks]**

2. Explain why rapidly increasing populations in tropical countries make sustainable forest management very challenging. **[2 marks]**

 **Made a start** **Feeling confident** **Exam ready**

Taiga forest characteristics

Taiga forests are in the low-energy, cold climate of the taiga biome. Unlike tropical rainforests, conditions for plant growth are poor. There is low biodiversity.

⑤ Plant and animal adaptations ✓

- Some animals migrate to warmer areas in winter, including most bird species.
- Other animals have small ears and short tails to avoid frostbite, or the ability to hibernate.
- The snowshoe hare has a brown summer coat, which turns white in the winter for camouflage against the snow. Red squirrels have fur that gets thicker in the winter.
- The taiga forest mainly consists of pine trees and other conifer species. These are evergreen trees, which do not drop their leaves in autumn, so they are ready to start photosynthesising as soon as spring comes.
- Conifers often have a cone-shaped structure, with branches sloping downwards. This means snow slides off them rather than building up and snapping off branches.
- Pine needles have a small surface area and a waxy coating that stops them losing water. They are dark green, which makes them capable of photosynthesising in low light levels. They contain very little sap, which means they do not contain much liquid to freeze in winter.

② Taiga forest characteristics ✓

- ☑ Winters are long and cold, with several months well below freezing.
- ☑ Summers are mild and very short.
- ☑ The taiga is quite dry: there is often less than 500 mm of precipitation per year.
- ☑ Taiga plants only grow during the short summer season, so biomass is low.
- ☑ The litter layer freezes in the winter, so there is no decomposition and there are low levels of nutrients.
- ☑ Only a few plant and animal species can survive the winter, so there is low biodiversity. Some species migrate to warmer areas, while a small number of species have special adaptations in order to survive.

⑤ Exam-style practice   Grades 4–6 ✓

Explain **one** way plants are adapted to climate conditions in the taiga. **[3 marks]**

⑩ Worked example   Grades 4–6 ✓

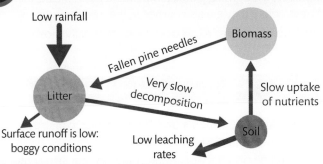

Figure 1 A taiga nutrient cycle diagram

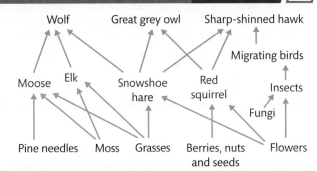

Figure 2 A food web for a Canadian taiga ecosystem

Study **Figure 1** and **Figure 2**, which show a nutrient cycle diagram and a food web diagram for a taiga ecosystem. Assess the differences between a taiga ecosystem and a tropical rainforest ecosystem. **[8 marks]**

Biodiversity is low in the taiga because it is a low productivity ecosystem, with little active nutrient cycling. The taiga is frozen for much of the year, with little daylight, so plants stop growing. This means there is very little vegetation to eat, and so only a few animal species, insulated by thick fur, are able to survive the taiga winters. This contrasts strongly with the tropical rainforest ecosystem, in which temperatures are very warm all year round, with high levels of rainfall. Consequently, plants in tropical rainforests grow all year, creating abundant food resources for a huge variety of life and making the rainforests the most biodiverse ecosystems on land.

Pine trees dominate the taiga forest ecosystem. They are well adapted to the cold, dry conditions. Their leaves are pine needles. These have a low surface area, reducing loss of water in the dry taiga conditions, and contain very little sap so that they do not freeze solid in winter. Only a few specialised animals, such as the moose, have adapted to eat pine needles. While the taiga does have more food available in summer from grasses, flowers and berries, this means that food webs in the taiga are very simple. This contrasts with the tropical rainforest, which has very complex food webs due to the high biodiversity and large biomass.

While the biggest nutrient store in the tropical rainforest is biomass, in the taiga it is the litter layer. This is because decomposition is very slow in the taiga, so nutrients build up in the litter layer and are not released into the soil to be absorbed by plants. In contrast, decomposition in the rainforest happens very rapidly in the warm, wet conditions, making nutrients quickly available for absorption.

Threats to taiga forest

The main direct threat to taiga forest is logging. Indirect threats include mining and the damage done by acid precipitation, forest fires, pests and diseases.

⑮ Direct and indirect threats

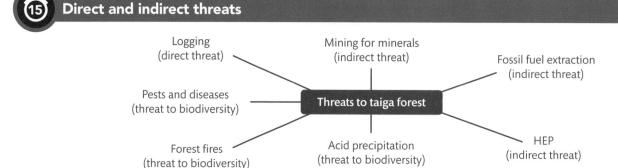

Logging (direct threat)

Mining for minerals (indirect threat)

Fossil fuel extraction (indirect threat)

Pests and diseases (threat to biodiversity)

Threats to taiga forest

Forest fires (threat to biodiversity)

Acid precipitation (threat to biodiversity)

HEP (indirect threat)

- **Logging** the taiga forest often involves clear-cutting whole areas of forest, which means cutting down every tree. The taiga forest is the main source of the world's softwood, which is used in pulp and paper production. Logging is a direct threat because it directly causes deforestation.

- **Mining for minerals or fossil fuels** becomes a threat when pollution escapes into the taiga forest ecosystem. Oil spills are very damaging because the low rate of decomposition means the oil remains in the ecosystem for a very long time without being broken down. Tree roots take up oil and this often kills the trees.

- **Exploiting hydroelectric power (HEP) potential** can result in entire valleys being flooded when dams are constructed.

- **Acid precipitation** happens when fossil fuels are burned, releasing sulphur dioxide and nitrogen oxides into the atmosphere. These chemicals combine with rainwater to produce weak acids that fall to earth as acid precipitation. The acid precipitation damages plant leaves and trees and kills insect eggs and microbes in the soil. This means there are fewer insects for other animals to eat, reducing biodiversity.

- **Forest fires** are becoming more frequent. Historically, some areas of taiga forest only experienced forest fires every 80–100 years. However, forest fires have become more common because of rising global temperatures. This means there is not enough time for slow-growing saplings to replace dead trees before they are also burned in the next forest fire.

- **New pests and diseases** are spreading into the taiga forest. Spruce-bark beetle kills taiga trees, especially those weakened by other threats such as acid precipitation.

⑤ Worked example   Grades 4–6

Figure 1 Oil pipelines in the taiga forest in Siberia, Russian Federation

Study **Figure 1**, which shows oil pipelines constructed through the taiga forest in Siberia.

Explain why the development of the oil industry in the taiga indirectly threatens the taiga forest. **[4 marks]**

Extracting oil has damaging consequences for the taiga forest ecosystem. For example, oil spills are a common problem in Russia, where the oil industry is not regulated very strictly. Oil spills pollute forest soils and poison trees. The oil industry also often burns off natural gas released from oil drilling. Sparks from this process can start forest fires, which are very damaging.

② Exam-style practice   Grades 4–6

Suggest **one** reason why climate change might be linked to the spread of new pests in the taiga forest.

[2 marks]

Made a start ☑   Feeling confident ☑   Exam ready ☑

Protecting the taiga forest

Setting up national parks and conservation areas effectively protects the taiga forest against many threats. However, there are conflicting views about protecting and exploiting the taiga's natural resources.

⑤ Wilderness areas and national parks

Although the taiga is the largest biome on the planet, it does not face the population pressures of the tropical rainforest because the taiga forest is not an easy place for humans to live.

- Much of the taiga forest is in **wilderness** areas. In North America, wilderness means government-owned land where it is not permitted to construct roads and buildings.
- National parks are open for recreational use, but the law prevents other exploitation of these areas.
- There is pressure to exploit oil and gas in taiga areas that have these resources, making the taiga more difficult to protect.
- The taiga is a fragile ecosystem that is easily damaged by pollution. This creates challenges for the management of national parks and wilderness areas.

Figure 1 A national park in Canada

⑤ Conflicting views

Arguments for protecting the taiga

- Clear-cutting wipes out entire habitats.
- Indigenous people live in the taiga. Exploitation threatens their way of life.
- The taiga is important on a global scale for absorbing and storing CO_2.
- Preserving the taiga gives people a chance to experience wilderness areas.

Figure 2 Logging in the taiga

Arguments for exploiting the taiga

- The economies of countries such as Canada and Russia rely on exploiting the taiga for oil and gas.
- Trees from the taiga are the world's main source of softwood, which is an industry worth billions of dollars.
- Exploiting the taiga can provide jobs and opportunities for people who live in taiga areas.

⑤ Worked example — Grades 4–6

Suggest **one** reason for opposition to sustainable forest management. **[2 marks]**

Business/industry might say that the sustainable forest management practice of leaving trees to grow and protecting them from being felled is wrong, because felling them could provide jobs for people living in the taiga forest and boost the country's economy.

planting · 18 years clearing · 120 years felling · 40–70 years thinning

Figure 3 A model of sustainable forest management

② Exam-style practice — Grades 4–6

Study **Figure 3**, which shows one model of sustainable forest management. Describe how sustainable forest management works. **[4 marks]**

Energy impacts

Energy resources can be classified as non-renewable, renewable or recyclable. All types of energy resource extraction or generation can have environmental or landscape impacts.

Types of energy resources

Non-renewable resources
- Sources of energy that are finite and will eventually run out – for example, oil, coal and gas (fossil fuels).
- They are often relatively cheap sources of energy.
- Burning fossil fuels produces large amounts of CO_2, contributing to global warming.

Renewable resources
- Renewable resources include wind, solar and wave energy.
- Unlike fossil fuels, renewable resources will not run out.
- Renewable energy resources depend on location. For example, solar panels need lots of sunshine to generate energy.

Recyclable resources
- Nuclear and biofuels are recyclable resources.
- Biofuels are produced from biomass, which can be regrown within a relatively short time through sustainable farming.
- Nuclear energy is produced from uranium, which can be reprocessed and reused.

Impacts of energy extraction

Land used for solar and wind farms cannot be used to produce food.

Road building and mining in forested areas causes deforestation, which has a number of negative environmental impacts.

Figure 1 The impacts of non-renewable and renewable energy extraction

Hydroelectric dams can flood large areas, destroying wildlife habitats.

Open-cast mining scars the landscape and increases carbon emissions.

Oil spills are very damaging, especially in cold environments. Oil kills marine life and birds.

② Exam-style practice   Grades 4–6

Explain **one** way in which using renewable energy resources reduces carbon emissions.   **[2 marks]**

Distribution of energy

You need to know the factors that influence the distribution of energy supply and consumption.

10 Variations in energy use

Energy consumption is increasing. Some experts predict that global energy consumption will continue to rise at approximately 2 per cent per year. This is equivalent to doubling consumption every 35 years. However, **Figure 1** shows that energy use per capita varies greatly between different countries.

Reasons for variation in energy consumption

- Levels of economic development are a significant factor in energy consumption. Developed countries tend to have high levels of energy use, because people have more money to buy electrical products and cars. In emerging countries, economic growth increases the demand for domestic and industrial energy.

- The size and composition of a country's economy also affects its energy consumption. The UK has a large economy, but the majority of this consists of tertiary and quaternary industry. This means that energy use per capita is comparatively low. Countries, such as India, whose economies are growing quickly through rapid industrialisation are likely to use more energy in manufacturing and production.

- Less developed countries tend to rely more heavily on traditional fuel sources for domestic energy, such as burning wood and other biomass. This results in a lower energy use per capita. For example, Africa is the continent where the lowest percentage of people have access to electricity, and in 2014 African countries had some of the lowest levels of energy use per capita. In South Sudan, energy use per capita was 60.73 kg of oil equivalent per capita, whereas in the United States it was 6956.81 kg of oil equivalent per capita.

5 What factors affect energy supply?

- **Climate** – areas with high levels of sunshine (e.g. Sahara Desert in Africa) can generate more energy from solar farms. Mountainous areas (e.g. Himalayas) that receive high levels of precipitation are suitable for the generation of HEP.

- **Geology** – some countries have abundant fossil fuels and geothermal energy resources. Geology also determines whether these resources are easily accessible or trapped beneath hard, resistant rock and difficult to extract. For example, Iceland's location in a tectonically active area, with many volcanoes, means the country has plenty of geothermal energy available.

- **Accessibility** – the nature of the landscape affects the accessibility of energy supplies. For example, hot (arid) deserts may seem ideal for generating solar energy, but this may not be possible if they are in remote or mountainous areas.

- **Technology** – less economically developed countries do not always have enough money to invest in energy generation, whereas more economically developed countries have had the money to invest in new technologies, which has enabled the extraction of new resources, such as shale and gas.

5 Worked example   Grades 1–3

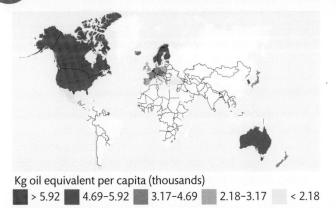

Kg oil equivalent per capita (thousands)
■ > 5.92 ■ 4.69–5.92 ■ 3.17–4.69 ■ 2.18–3.17 □ < 2.18

Figure 1 Energy use in 2014

Study **Figure 1**, which shows energy use in 2014 (kg of oil equivalent per capita).

Which of the following countries had an energy use of more than 5920 kg per capita?

[1 mark]

☐ **A** France
☒ **B** Canada
☐ **C** Australia
☐ **D** Japan

5 Exam-style practice   Grade 5

Describe how a reliance on traditional fuel sources (e.g. burning wood) may affect energy use per capita.   **[2 marks]**

Oil and the economy

Oil is essential to our modern way of life. Global demand for oil is increasing, but oil resources are unevenly distributed and prices are affected by changing international relations and economic factors.

(5) Oil production

- The production of oil is increasing to meet growing demand for oil around the world.
- Many countries, such as Japan and China, do not have oil reserves and have to import oil.
- Although oil reserves in some countries are running out, there are major reserves in South America, Africa and the Arctic that have not been developed.
- Five countries are responsible for almost half of the world's oil production: the USA, Saudi Arabia, Russia, China and Canada.

Global oil consumption is increasing as countries develop and their economies grow. However, like production, consumption is uneven.

Exam focus

To work out a percentage increase or decrease, find the difference between the two numbers you are comparing, divide this number by the original number and multiply the answer by 100. For a percentage decrease, the answer will be a negative number.

(5) Oil prices

The small number of countries that produce oil and the huge demand for oil around the world have important consequences. Oil prices are affected by economic factors and changing international relations.

- **Oversupply and undersupply** affect price. If oil-producing countries join together, they can decide to produce less oil to make prices rise, or produce more oil if prices are rising too high.
- **Recessions**, such as the one that began in 2008, reduce demand for oil and oil prices fall.
- **Conflict** in oil-producing countries such as Iraq makes oil prices rise, because it affects supply.
- **Diplomatic relations** between countries can create uncertainty that affects oil prices.

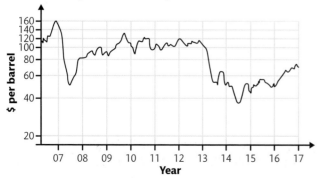

Figure 2 The price of crude oil in US dollars per barrel from 2007 to 2017

(2) Oil consumption

Oil consumption by region (million barrels per day)

Key:
- Asia Pacific
- Africa
- Middle East
- Europe and Eurasia
- South and Central America
- North America

Figure 1 Oil consumption by world region (1991–2016)

(5) Worked example — Grades 4–6

1 Study **Figure 1**, which shows global oil consumption by region. Calculate the percentage increase in consumption from 1991 to 2016.
[2 marks]

$96 - 67 = 29$

$\frac{29}{67} \times 100 = 43.28\%$

2 Explain why oil consumption has grown fastest in the Asia Pacific region. **[4 marks]**

Oil consumption increases as countries industrialise, because they need energy for factories, as well as fuel for transport to move and export manufactured products. China has industrialised rapidly since the 1990s, so a lot of the increase in consumption in Asia probably comes from China's industrialisation.

A second reason could be rising GDP. As people in the Asia Pacific region have moved from the countryside to work in factories, they have earned more money. They can now afford things that require energy, such as cars, fridges and air conditioning. This increases the demand for energy, especially oil.

(2) Exam-style practice — Grades 4–6

Study **Figure 2**, which shows changes in the price of oil between 2007 and 2017.

Suggest **one** reason for the sudden drop in the price of oil in 2007. **[2 marks]**

 Made a start **Feeling confident** **Exam ready**

Conventional and unconventional oil and gas

Increasing demand for energy can make it worth extracting oil and gas from remote and challenging locations. This has economic costs and benefits. Increasing demand also makes it profitable to develop unconventional sources of oil and gas such as tar sands and shale gas, but this has environmental costs.

 ## Economic impacts

According to the US Geological Survey, the Arctic contains the last major reserves of oil in the world, with approximately 412 billion barrels of oil equivalent. However, the Arctic, one of the last great wildernesses on Earth, is isolated and extremely cold. It is home to species such as whales, walruses and polar bears, all of which are endangered.

Exploiting the Arctic for oil can have economic costs and benefits.

- US President Donald Trump passed a law at the end of 2017 which permitted drilling for oil in the Arctic National Wildlife Refuge. He claims it will generate $1 billion over the next 10 years.
- However, exploring for oil in the Arctic is expensive. The extreme cold and the isolated location require companies to construct infrastructure and invest in specialist equipment.
- Shell, a transnational corporation (TNC), began drilling for oil in the Alaskan Arctic but stopped in 2015 after widespread public opposition to the potential for environmental damage, such as oil spills. The company had spent over £4.5 billion on its search for oil.

 ## Environmental costs

Unconventional sources of oil and gas include extracting oil from tar sands and extracting shale gas, a process known as fracking.

The environmental costs of developing unconventional oil and gas sources include:

- possible deforestation in environmentally sensitive areas
- release of very large amounts of carbon dioxide
- pollution of rivers, lakes and groundwater, because of the chemicals used in the high-pressure water used for fracking
- destruction of precious wildlife habitats
- air and noise pollution.

Shale gas extraction

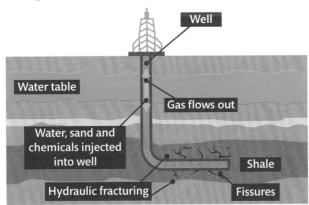

Figure 1 Shale gas extraction works by drilling into shale rock and pumping a mixture of water, sand and chemicals into the shale layer at high pressure. This fractures the rocks, releasing shale gas, which is collected at the surface.

 ## Worked example — Grades 4–6

Study **Figure 1**, which shows the process of shale gas extraction.

Explain why shale gas extraction can have environmental costs. **[4 marks]**

Fracking (shale gas extraction) requires a lot of water. Taking this water from local rivers could have environmental costs such as loss of habitat for river life. Transporting water to fracking locations would also use up a lot of energy because water is heavy. This would increase greenhouse gas emissions. The chemicals used in fracking might also escape into the ecosystem, for example into groundwater or rivers, and these chemicals could pollute the water and damage local ecosystems. Finally, shale gas is a fossil fuel, so burning it for energy releases very large amounts of carbon dioxide, which contributes to climate change.

 ## Exam-style practice — Grades 4–6

Tar sands are made of a heavy, sticky type of oil called bitumen mixed with sand and clay. They are usually extracted in open-cast mines, and then the sand is heated to extract the oil.

Explain **one** possible environmental cost of extracting oil from tar sands. **[2 marks]**

 Made a start — **Feeling confident** — **Exam ready**

Reducing fossil fuel reliance

You need to know about the importance of energy efficiency and conservation, and the costs and benefits of fossil fuel alternatives.

 ## Sustainable energy options

The following measures will help reduce energy demand and carbon emissions, so finite fossil fuel supplies last longer.

Transport
Energy efficiency refers to getting as much useful power from as little energy as possible. For example, cars are now more aerodynamic and have improved engine efficiency (they can travel further on the same amount of fuel) resulting in energy conservation and reduced emissions.

Energy conservation at home
Individuals can conserve energy at home and reduce demand by:
• using energy-efficient light bulbs
• not leaving TVs and laptops on standby
• switching off appliances at the wall when they're not being used
• lowering the thermostat to reduce energy used for heating.

Sustainable energy options

Individual use/carbon footprints
We can all reduce carbon emissions by car sharing, using public transport, recycling, buying local produce (with fewer food miles) and reducing waste.

Energy efficiency at home
Individuals can conserve energy at home and reduce demand, for example by lowering the thermostat to reduce energy used for heating.

 ## Costs and benefits of renewable energy

Type of resource	Benefits	Costs
Biofuels are produced from organic matter that is replaceable within a short period.	👍 Biofuels are renewable fuels produced from plant or animal waste (e.g. ethanol, biogas and methanol). 👍 It is possible to generate energy from organic matter, such as used cooking oil. 👍 Biofuels produce less CO_2 than fossil fuels.	✊ A finite amount of land is suitable for growing crops, and land used to grow crops for biofuel cannot be used for food. Global demand for both energy and food is rising. ✊ Irrigating crops for biofuels, such as corn for producing bioethanol, uses large volumes of water.
Wind turbines convert air movement into electricity.	👍 Turbines do not produce any greenhouse gases or air pollution. 👍 Wind power could meet a large percentage of global energy demands. 👍 Turbines are space efficient. Agricultural land between turbines can still be used productively.	✊ Turbines use land that could otherwise be used for food crops or housing. ✊ Wind is unpredictable and many locations are not suitable for turbines. ✊ They can harm wildlife: birds and bats are killed by wind turbine blades.
Solar power is generated by converting the Sun's energy into electricity.	👍 The Sun's energy will not run out. 👍 Solar panels do not produce greenhouse gases or air, water or noise pollution. 👍 Solar has few environmental impacts compared to other renewables such as HEP. 👍 It can be used to generate both heat and electricity.	✊ Solar power plants use land that could otherwise be used for food crops or housing. ✊ Solar panels are expensive to install. ✊ Supply depends on climate and time of day, and stops at night. Some areas of the world are better suited for generating solar power than others.
Hydroelectric power (HEP) is electricity generated using energy from falling water.	👍 HEP is a clean fuel source that does not cause air pollution or emit greenhouse gases. 👍 It is a reliable source of power, without the fluctuations of solar or wind. 👍 The reservoirs behind hydroelectric dams can provide an extra source of water for drinking or irrigating crops.	✊ A finite number of sites are suitable for generating HEP. ✊ HEP sites that use water trapped behind a dam to generate electricity can flood very large areas. This may result in the displacement of people from the area. It can also harm or destroy river ecosystems.

 ## Worked example   Grades 1–2

Explain **one** technical challenge of using hydrogen as an alternative to fossil fuel.   **[2 marks]**

Hydrogen for fuel is stored at high pressure as a super-cooled liquid. This makes it a dangerous fuel to use because if it leaked and got onto human skin it would cause severe frostbite.

All types of renewable energy have an impact on the environment, e.g. carbon emissions during construction, energy to make construction materials.

 ## Exam-style practice   Grade 5

Explain why hydroelectric power has both costs and benefits.   **[4 marks]**

     Made a start   **Feeling confident**   **Exam ready**

Attitudes to energy futures

Current energy use is not sustainable, but moving towards a sustainable future for energy production and energy consumption requires big changes.

② Changing attitudes to energy

In some developed countries, such as Scandinavian countries and the UK, attitudes are changing away from a 'business as usual' approach, and towards lowering carbon emissions, reducing consumption and increasing reliance on renewables.

Reasons for changing attitudes to energy include:

- **Rising affluence** – as people become wealthier, they can afford initially expensive options such as solar panels.
- **Environmental concerns** – more people want to protect the natural world and its plant and animal species. This can be influenced by campaigns from environmental groups, such as WWF.
- **Education** – an educated population that understands the causes of climate change can make informed choices about energy futures.

⑤ Worked example — Grades 4–6

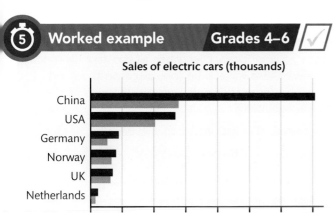

Sales of electric cars (thousands)

■ Jan–April, 2018 ■ Jan–April, 2017

Figure 1 Sales of electric cars (in thousands of cars) in the first three months of 2018 compared to the first three months of 2017

Study **Figure 1**, which shows electric car sales between January and April in 2017 and 2018. Suggest **two** reasons for the increase in electric car sales. **[4 marks]**

One reason may be education. People in these countries learn about unsustainable energy use and its impact on the environment and they may decide to make a change in their lifestyle to reduce their carbon footprint.

Another reason could be oil prices. People who are well-off may decide that although electric cars are much more expensive to buy than petrol cars, they can afford to buy one and make long-term savings on fuel.

⑩ Views about energy futures

Climate scientists have provided a range of evidence that the use of fossil fuels is causing global warming, and that this is already having a significant impact on the environment and on people's lives. However, there are conflicting views in society between moving towards a more sustainable energy future and prioritising business and consumer needs by continuing with 'business as usual'.

- Environmentalists argue that countries around the world must move from non-renewable to renewable sources of energy and from unsustainable to sustainable energy use.
- Many governments around the world have agreed to reduce their reliance on fossil fuels, generate more renewable energy, and improve the efficiency of energy use, for example by changing street lighting from lightbulbs to more energy-efficient LEDs.
- However, governments are under pressure from consumers and businesses, who do not want to pay more for the energy they use. This includes pressure from transnational corporations (TNCs), which can move production to other countries with cheaper power.

⑤ Carbon footprints

- A carbon footprint is the total amount of carbon dioxide and other greenhouse gases released into the atmosphere as a result of individual, organisation or community activities.
- It is stated as kilograms (kg) of equivalent CO_2.
- The world average is around 4000 kg per person, the UK average was 7000 kg per person in 2017, and the target for sustainable energy use is 2000 kg per person.
- Methods for reducing carbon footprints include flying less, insulating homes, using efficient heating and air conditioning methods, and eating less meat.

Rearing sheep and cows uses a lot of carbon. Livestock also emit methane, a greenhouse gas.

⑤ Exam-style practice — Grades 4–6

Environmentalists advocate the sustainable use of energy. Suggest **two** reasons why TNCs might not agree.

[4 marks]

Exam skills: Geographical issues

Paper 3 of your Geography exam is a decision-making paper. The questions will be based on resources in a Resource Booklet and the three People and Environment Issues topics you have studied.

Paper 3 structure

Paper 3 is divided into sections:
- Sections A and B have short answer questions (worth up to 4 marks).
- Section C has short answer questions and 8-mark extended answer questions.
- Section D has a 12-mark extended writing question (plus 4 marks for SPaG).

Topics in Paper 3

Paper 3 covers the following topics.
- People and the biosphere (pages 72–73)
- Forests under threat (pages 74–79)
- Consuming energy resources (pages 80–85)

The Resource Booklet

You will be given a Resource Booklet in Paper 3 of your exam, which will include a variety of resources. These may include fact files, maps, graphs and tables. Skim the Resource Booklet before you look at the questions, but do not read it in detail until you have read the questions. **Figure 1** below, a fact file, is an example of a resource you might be given in your Resource Booklet.

Figure 1
Coal mining in Northumberland

A company called Banks Mining plans to open a new open-cast coal mine near Druridge Bay, in Northumberland. Open-cast mining involves extracting coal by removing the surface soil and rocks, and digging out the coal underneath. The company intend to extract coal between 2016 and 2027 and plan to restore the site to its former beauty.

- The open-cast mine will create over 100 full-time jobs.
- The site will become a visitor attraction when restored.
- Coal from Druridge Bay might be used in UK power stations, reducing imports and keeping an estimated £200 000 in the UK economy.

Location of mining area

Druridge Bay is on the north-east coast of the UK, between the villages of Ellington and Widdrington. The site contains 7 million tonnes of coal, which will take around 10 years to extract.

Worked example Grades 5–9

Study **Figure 1**, which gives information about a proposed coal mine in Northumberland.
Using evidence from the resource, assess the local and national economic benefits of developing the coal mine. **[8 marks]**

> This is an example of an 8-mark extended answer question in Paper 3, Section C. Use **Figure 1** below to answer this question.

Developing the coal mine could bring 100 jobs to the local area. The fact file says the coal mine is located between two villages so it is probably in a rural area. Rural areas do not have very many job opportunities outside farming, so the 100 jobs will probably have a very big impact, bigger than if it was an urban area. Even when all the coal has been mined, there will still be jobs because there will be work in restoring the environment and at the visitor centre.

There are also national economic benefits, because the coal mined at Druridge Bay can be used in UK power stations. The power stations will be spending money on UK-mined energy instead of foreign coal. However, the benefit might not be that significant nationally, for two main reasons. Firstly, Banks Mining may not be a UK company. They could be a TNC with headquarters in another country, or they may be a company with a lot of FDI. The owners of UK power stations might also be foreign companies. This could mean that money made by selling coal to UK power stations would not all stay in the UK. Secondly, coal produced in the UK is likely to be more expensive than coal from other countries, where wages are a lot lower. Even the cost of transporting the coal to the UK does not make it more expensive than UK coal – this is why coal mines have closed in the UK over the last 50 years.

While the local economic benefits are likely to be valuable, therefore, the national benefits of coal mining at Druridge Bay may turn out to be less valuable.

Exam-style practice Grades 5–9

Study **Figure 1**. Explain **one** benefit of open-cast coal mining in Northumberland. **[2 marks]**

   Made a start   **Feeling confident**   **Exam ready**

Making a geographical decision

The extended writing question in Section D is worth 16 marks, including 4 for SPaG. You will need to make and justify a decision about a geographical issue using information from the Resource Booklet and your knowledge and understanding from your whole geography course.

⑤ Examples of decision-making options

If your Resource Booklet contained different resources about sustainable energy in the UK and consumer opinions about energy, the three options for the decision-making question could be similar to these.

Study the **three** options below for how the UK should develop its energy in the future.

Option 1: Take non-renewable and nuclear energy production off line and switch entirely to renewable sources of energy for the UK.

Option 2: Build more nuclear power stations around the UK, so the country can depend on reliable nuclear energy. Phase out non-renewable energy; use renewables when available to top-up nuclear.

Option 3: Continue to use a mix of energy sources, both renewable and non-renewable, including the development of shale gas.

⑩ Worked example   Grades 5–9

Select the option that you think would be the best **long-term** plan for how Britain's energy should be generated in the future. Justify your choice.
Use knowledge and understanding from the rest of your geography course to support your answer. **[16 marks]**
Chosen option: 2

This is an extract from an answer. The complete answer should take around 20 minutes to write.

Building more nuclear power stations around the UK is the best way to make sure the UK has a sustainable energy future, because nuclear power is reliable but has very low carbon emissions. This means that the UK could use renewables when conditions were suitable for wind and solar, but continue to have reliable power from nuclear sources as a back-up.

Refer to the Resource Booklet to provide specific examples that justify your decision.

Figure 5 in the Resource Booklet shows the low level of carbon emissions from nuclear power: while coal causes $900\,g$ of CO_2 emissions per kWh, emissions from nuclear power can be as low as $10\,g$ per kWh.

Consider the advantages and disadvantages of the other options, and use them to justify the option you have chosen.

Option 1 is the most sustainable, because nuclear power does have disadvantages, especially the cost of building new power stations. As Figure 6 shows, the cost of building Hinkley Point C is estimated at £20 billion, which the figure says could be used instead to build 40 new hospitals. However, the problem with Option 1 is that UK consumers and businesses want to have electricity available at all times. Although the UK is often considered to be the windiest country in Europe (mostly due to Scotland, which is one of the ten windiest countries in the world), it is not windy all the time. It therefore needs another constant, reliable energy source. Since Option 1 has no kind of back-up for when it is dark and calm, meaning there is no solar or wind energy, it is not a practical option.

Try to include your own knowledge, such as the disadvantages of solar and wind energy.

4 marks are available for SPaG, so remember to be accurate in your spelling, punctuation and grammar. Use specialist terms such as 'fracking', 'fossil fuels' and 'sustainable' accurately.

Option 3 is the 'business as usual' option – the UK currently has a mix of renewables and non-renewables, although without shale gas. Fracking would give the UK the potential to generate a lot more of its own energy, as the USA has done. However, I do not think that the UK should continue to rely on fossil fuels because the impacts of climate change caused by the enhanced greenhouse effect make it unsustainable in the long term…

⑳ Exam-style practice   Grades 5–9

Look at the options at the top of this page. Select the option that you think would be the best **long-term** plan for how Britain's energy should be generated in the future. Justify your choice.

Use knowledge and understanding from the rest of your geography course to support your answer. **[16 marks]**

 Made a start   **Feeling confident**   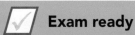 **Exam ready**

Working with maps and atlases

Geographers use different types of maps to identify distributions and patterns of human and physical features. You need to know how to identify and describe different geographical features using maps at global, national and local scales.

(5) Lines of latitude and longitude ✓

Lines of **latitude** and **longitude** are used to locate places accurately.

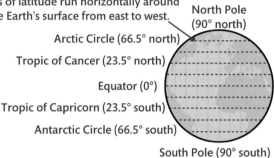

Lines of latitude run horizontally around the Earth's surface from east to west.

North Pole (90° north)
Arctic Circle (66.5° north)
Tropic of Cancer (23.5° north)
Equator (0°)
Tropic of Capricorn (23.5° south)
Antarctic Circle (66.5° south)
South Pole (90° south)

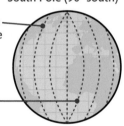

Lines of longtitude (meridians) run vertically and meet at a point at the North and South Poles. They are measurements east and west of the Prime Meridian.

Prime meridian (or Greenwich Meridian) at 0° longitude.

Figure 1 Lines of latitude and longitude

The International Date Line, which separates calendar dates (when you cross it, the date changes), roughly follows 180° longitude.

A **distribution** refers to the way geographical features are spread out or arranged. Atlases contain a wide range of maps showing the distribution of key geographical factors on a world scale.

Geographical skills

Use **PQE** to describe a distribution on a map.

P – Give the general **pattern**.

Q – **Quantify** (support) the pattern with evidence taken directly from the map.

E – Identify any **exceptions** to the pattern (anomalies).

A **pattern** is a way of showing a connection between geographical features.

When describing patterns of geographical features on a map you can use key terms such as linear (along a line), dispersed (spread out) and nucleated (close together).

(5) Worked example Grades 4–5 ✓

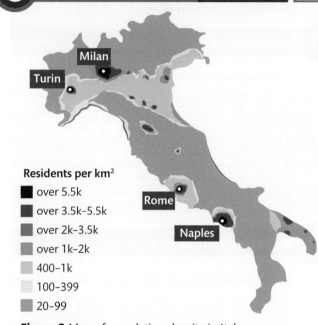

Residents per km²
- over 5.5k
- over 3.5k–5.5k
- over 2k–3.5k
- over 1k–2k
- 400–1k
- 100–399
- 20–99

Figure 2 Map of population density in Italy

Study **Figure 2,** which shows population density in Italy. Describe the distribution shown on the map. **[3 marks]**

The map shows that the areas of highest population density are concentrated around the cities of Turin, Milan, Rome and Naples, all of which include areas of more than 3.5 thousand people per square kilometre. Generally, the areas of lowest population density are in the centre of the country, with large areas of 20–99 people per square kilometre, whilst there is higher population density in the north-east of the country.

(5) Exam-style practice Grades 4–5 ✓

Eurasian plate
North American plate
Eurasian plate
Pacific plate
African plate
South American plate
Indo-Australian plate
Antarctic plate

— plate boundary
• earthquakes

Figure 3 The distribution of earthquakes

Study **Figure 3**, which shows earthquake distribution and plate boundaries. Describe the global pattern of earthquakes. **[2 marks]**

✓ **Made a start** ✓ **Feeling confident** ✓ **Exam ready**

Coordinates, scale and distance

You need to know how to use four- and six-figure grid references to find features on a map, be able to measure distances and understand scale.

 Geographical skills

Using grid references

- To work out the **four-figure grid reference** of the shaded square, move east using the vertical lines (eastings) from the left edge of the map until you reach the left edge of the square. This is the first number, **33**. Then move from the bottom of the map northwards using the horizontal lines (northings) until you reach the bottom of the square. This is the second number, **81**. Therefore, the four-figure grid reference of the shaded square is **3381**.
- To work out the **six-figure grid reference** of the church with a tower, imagine that the grid squares are divided by lines into ten equal sections horizontally and vertically. Picturing the ten vertical lines, move east from the left edge of the square, **330**, to where the church symbol is, **335**. Then in the same way, move up from the bottom edge of the square, **810**, to the church at **815**. The six-figure grid reference for the church with a tower is **335815**.

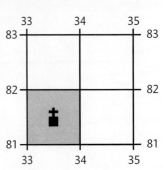

Figure 1 A simple grid

Measuring distances

For your exam, you could be asked to work out two types of distances using an OS map:

- **straight line distances,** such as a straight part of a road
- **curved line distances,** such as meanders along a river.

You will need a ruler to measure both types of distance and a piece of string to measure curved line distances.

You will then need to convert the measurement using the **scale** on the map. The scale tells you how much smaller the area shown on the map is compared to the actual area. If you measure a road as 6 cm long on a map with the scale 1:50 000, the road is actually 3 km long, as 1 cm on the map is the equivalent to 500 m. However, if you measure a road as 6 cm long on a map with the scale 1:25 000, it means the road is 1.5 km long, as 1 cm on the map equals 250 m – a completely different answer.

 Worked example **Grade 7**

1 Identify the feature located at reference 593244 on the map. **[1 mark]**

Castle

2 Identify the six-figure grid reference of the church near Bridstow. **[1 mark]**

585248

3 Calculate the approximate curved-line distance (in km) from the public house to the roundabout along the A49. **[2 marks]**

2 km

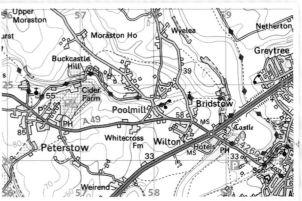

Figure 2 An OS map extract. Each of the grid squares is 2 cm by 2 cm, and the scale of the map is 1:50 000.

 Practice **Grades 4–5**

Study **Figure 2**.

(a) State the four-figure grid reference for Whitecross Farm. **[1 mark]**

(b) State the six-figure grid reference for the campsite south of Buckcastle Hill. **[1 mark]**

(c) State the straight line distance (in km) from Poolmill to Wyelea. **[1 mark]**

 Made a start 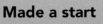 **Feeling confident** **Exam ready**

Cross sections and contours

Geographers use cross sections to provide a visual representation of the relief and key features of a landscape. You need to know how to interpret a cross section and relate a cross-sectional drawing to relief features on a map.

⑤ **OS maps features** ✓

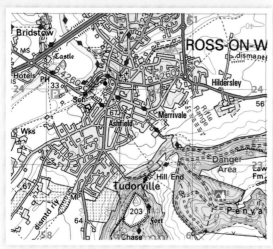

Figure 1 An OS map extract. Each of the grid squares is 2 cm by 2 cm, and the scale of the map is 1:50000.

- **Contour lines** on maps indicate points of equal height above sea level. They are 10 m apart on 1:50000 maps, and indicate the shape, size and height of key geographical features, such as river valleys and glacial landscape features.

- The distance between the contour lines represents the **gradient** of a slope. The closer the contour lines, the steeper the slope.

- You can identify **relief patterns** on a map by looking at contour lines. For example, an area of widely and evenly spaced contours, with areas of more closely packed contours either side suggests a river valley.

- Black dots with a number represent **spot heights**. The number shows the height, in metres, above sea level.

⑤ **Worked example**   **Grade 2** ✓

① Study **Figure 1**, which shows an extract from an OS map.

Identify the six-figure grid reference of the triangulation pillar.   **[1 mark]**

603225

② Describe what is shown by contour lines.   **[2 marks]**

Points of equal height above sea level

⑩ **Drawing a cross section** ✓

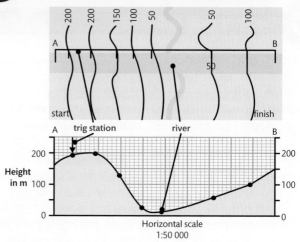

Figure 2 A cross section

① Place a piece of paper along the chosen line.

② Mark where the contour lines meet the transect line and label the heights.

③ Mark the location of key geographical features such as rivers and roads.

④ Draw the axes for your graph, making the horizontal line the same length as the transect line.

⑤ Place your piece of paper over the horizontal line and mark each of the contour values on the graph with a cross.

⑥ Join up the crosses and label the location of any key features.

② **Exam focus** 📌 ✓

Remember, map skills can be tested in any of your exam papers. You also need to be able draw on your knowledge of physical landscapes (pages 34–53 in this book) when interpreting map extracts in the exam.

Exam focus 📌

For your exam, make sure you can confidently understand and use contours and grid references.

② **Exam-style practice**   **Grade 2** ✓

Study **Figure 1**, which shows an extract from an OS map. State the height above sea level of the triangulation pillar.   **[1 mark]**

Settlement site, situation and shape

You need to be able to interpret the site, situation and shape of a settlement and identify different land use types from an OS map.

 Land use, site and situation ✓

- Wide areas of flat land without buildings or trees often indicate agricultural land use. Closely grouped buildings on a map show that the land is used for a settlement.
- The **site** of a settlement refers to the actual land on which a settlement is built.
- The **situation** is the settlement's location in relation to other features (human (e.g. roads) and physical (e.g. rivers)).
- Both physical and human factors that affect the site and situation of settlements can be interpreted from an OS map.

The castle suggests this was once a defensive site.

These contour lines show raised land, so the settlement is above the flood plain.

This land is flat with no buildings or trees, so it is probably used for farming.

Figure 1 Features of an OS map tell you about land use and the site and situation of a settlement.

 Shape ✓

There are three main types of settlement shape: dispersed, nucleated and linear.

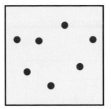 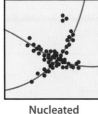 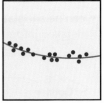

Dispersed   Nucleated   Linear

Figure 2 The three types of settlement shape

 Worked example   **Grades 3–4** ✓

Figure 3 An aerial photo of Hutton Conyers village, North Yorkshire.

Study **Figure 3**, which shows an aerial photo of a settlement.

Identify the main land use around the settlement.

[1 mark]

Large fields for pastoral and arable farming.

 Exam-style practice   **Grades 4–6** ✓

Study **Figure 3**, which shows an aerial photo of a settlement.
Describe the situation of the settlement.

[2 marks]

Sketch maps and annotations

You need to be able to label and annotate different types of diagrams, maps and photos, and sketch maps.

(10) Drawing sketch maps

In your exam, you might be asked to draw a sketch from a map or photograph. You might also produce sketch maps as part of your fieldwork. Sketch maps:

- show where key features are located
- have simple labels
- are often drawn from a birds-eye view (from above)
- can be annotated to add further explanation or more detailed information.

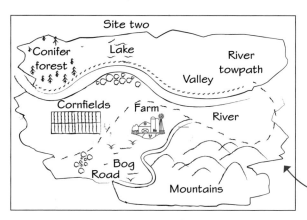

Figure 1 A sketch map from a bird's-eye view

(5) Sketching, labelling and annotating

You need to be able to label and annotate photos and sketches.

- A **label** is a word or short phrase that identifies a feature.
- An **annotation** is a sentence that explains something.
- Only label and annotate the features that are relevant to the question.
- When drawing a sketch, draw a frame (box) first and then draw your sketch inside it.
- Don't create a work of art – keep your sketch simple and use labels to make it clear what the features are.

Annotated diagrams are an effective way of answering questions about the stages in a process, such as the stages of coastal erosion or waterfall formation. Numbering the stages shows them in the correct sequence.

Geographical skills

When you carry out fieldwork, sketching a map of the area can help you remember the key features and layout of the landscape.

(5) Worked example   Grades 4–6

Study **Figure 2**, which is an aerial photo of a river. Explain the formation of feature X.

Figure 2 An aerial photo of a river

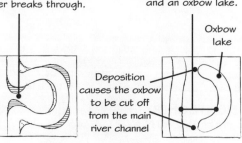

Erosion can cause both sides of a meander to migrate towards each other.

erosion

meander

deposition

The neck becomes narrower until the river breaks through.

This forms a straighter channel and an oxbow lake.

Oxbow lake

Deposition causes the oxbow to be cut off from the main river channel

Use a labelled diagram in your answer.

(5) Exam-style practice   Grades 4–6

Describe the structure of a tropical cyclone.   **[3 marks]**

Made a start   Feeling confident   Exam ready

Graphs and charts

In the exam, you could be asked to complete or interpret different types of graphs and charts. You need to know how to choose the most appropriate graph or chart to represent different types of data.

Line charts

A line chart represents continuous data that shows how something changes over time, such as population size. To accurately interpret a line chart, use a ruler to find the values on the x-axis and the y-axis.

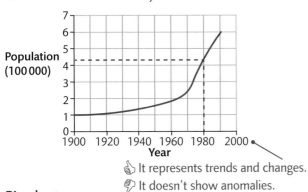

👍 It represents trends and changes.

👎 It doesn't show anomalies.

Pie charts

A pie chart represents proportions, such as a country's sources of energy.

If you are asked to complete a pie chart, you will need to find the angle of the segment. For instance, to work out the segment for coal, you need to find 20% of 360°.

$20 \div 100 = 0.2$

$0.2 \times 360° = 72°$

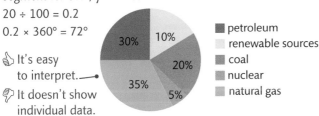

- petroleum
- renewable sources
- coal
- nuclear
- natural gas

👍 It's easy to interpret.

👎 It doesn't show individual data.

Pictograms

A pictogram represents data in a visual format with symbols. You read them in a similar way to a bar chart.

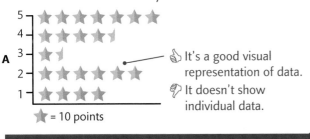

⭐ = 10 points

👍 It's a good visual representation of data.

👎 It doesn't show individual data.

See page 98 for how to extrapolate and interpolate data.

Bar charts

A bar chart represents discontinuous, generally numerical data that can be used when making comparisons, such as greenhouse gas emissions by country.

A divided bar chart can present multiple types of data.

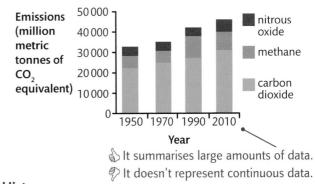

- nitrous oxide
- methane
- carbon dioxide

👍 It summarises large amounts of data.

👎 It doesn't represent continuous data.

Histograms

A histogram shows frequencies of groups of data, for instance the number of visitors that visit national parks each day.

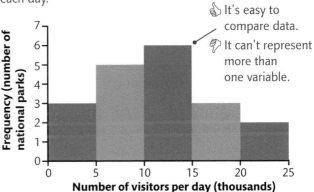

👍 It's easy to compare data.

👎 It can't represent more than one variable.

Scattergraphs

A scattergraph shows the relationship between two sets of data, such as rainfall and temperature. A **line of best fit** through the middle of the points is used to estimate other values.

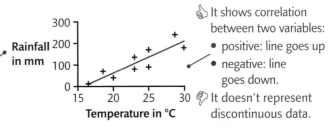

👍 It shows correlation between two variables:
- positive: line goes up
- negative: line goes down.

👎 It doesn't represent discontinuous data.

1 Would a line graph or bar chart be most suitable for presenting a set of discontinuous data? **[1 mark]**

2 State whether the scattergraph above shows a positive or negative correlation. **[1 mark]**

3 State **two** types of graph that are suitable for presenting continuous data. **[2 marks]**

 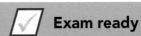

Maps and pyramids

In the exam, you might be asked to complete or interpret choropleth maps, flow-line maps and population pyramids. You need to know the advantages and disavantages of each type.

 Types of maps and pyramids

Choropleth maps

A choropleth map represents data using different shades of colours. It is a useful way of showing how data, such as population density, can vary over a geographical area.

👍 It provides a good visual representation of data.

👎 It shows abrupt changes across boundaries, but in reality boundaries merge.

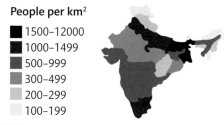

People per km²

- 1500–12000
- 1000–1499
- 500–999
- 300–499
- 200–299
- 100–199

Dot maps

A dot map can represent distribution, or how a value changes between geographical areas, such as population density. In the map below, each dot represents the same number of people. The more dots in a given area, the more people.

👍 It provides a good visual representation of data.

👎 Clusters of dots make it difficult to interpret data.

● = 500 000

Isoline maps

An isoline map shows lines that link all the points on a map where there is an equal value to demonstrate a pattern over a large geographical area. They are often used to show data relating to weather. Contour lines, used to show relief and the shape of landforms, are a type of isoline.

👍 Changes can be easily identified.

👎 It requires large amounts of data for the map to be accurate.

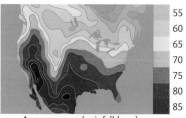

Average annual rainfall (mm)

Population pyramids

Population pyramids provide an overview of an area's population characteristics, including gender and age group.

👍 The general shape can provide quick access to data trends.

👎 Some detail is lost in data groups.

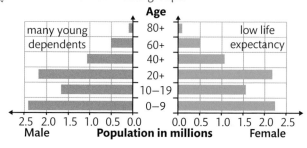

Flow-line maps

A flow-line map uses arrows to represent the size of a variable and the direction of movement, often the movement of people and goods between areas or countries.

👍 The scale and width of lines can be used to add extra detail.

👎 Distance and direction may not be represented accurately.

Immigration to the Unites States

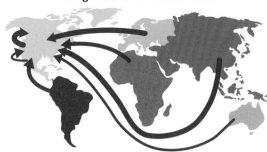

Proportional symbols maps

A proportional symbols map uses different sized shapes to represent data. The size of the symbol relates to the size of what is being represented.

👍 It's a good way of representing changing values.

👎 It can be difficult to produce.

Forestry production in million cubic meters

- 65
- 30
- 15
- 5

 Practice Grades 2–4

Study the population pyramid. Calculate the total number of male and females in the 10-19 age group. **[1 mark]**

✓ **Made a start** ✓ **Feeling confident** ✓ **Exam ready**

Using photos

You need to be able to use and interpret aerial, oblique, ground and satellite photos of a range of different landscapes.

 Biosphere services

1 Ground-level photos are the most commonly used photos. They capture foreground details such as historic buildings and waterfalls.

2 Aerial photos are usually taken from helicopters or drones looking down on the landscape. They can be vertical (looking directly down to the ground) or oblique (giving a sideways view of the landscape from above).

3 Satellite photos are images of the surface of the Earth. They measure visible light, water vapour or infrared radiation. Satellite images can be digitally enhanced to make features appear more prominent. They can also be used to show vegetation or settlement patterns.

Figure 1 A satellite image of the Earth

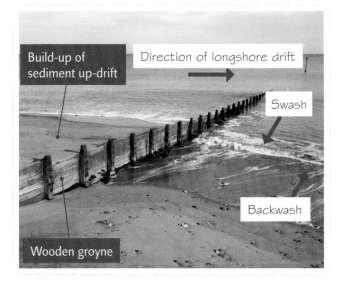

Figure 2 Ground-level photographs can be taken during fieldwork, using a camera or mobile device. They need to be annotated (handwriting) or labelled to show any features.

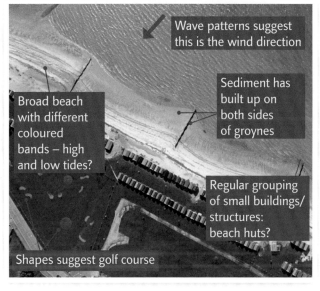

Figure 3 Aerial photos cover a wider area than ground-level photos, so they are useful in showing spatial patterns.

 Worked example   Grade 4

Suggest **one** benefit of using satellite photos.
[2 marks]

Satellite photos provide information from above, often over a wider area than ground-level photos.

 Exam focus

You may be asked to use a photo in combination with an OS map. You may be asked to describe geographical features shown, or identify the direction from which it was taken.

 Exam-style practice   Grades 4–6

Study **Figure 3**, which shows an annotated aerial photo.

Suggest **one** other piece of evidence from **Figure 3** that supports the annotations made on it about the direction of longshore drift.
[2 marks]

 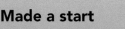

Interpreting patterns from GIS

Geographic Information Systems (GIS) provide layers of data about a location, usually on a base map of the location.

(10) Layers of data

Figure 1 An online flood risk map showing areas affected by previous flooding in Newborough (near Peterborough) in eastern England.

Make links between patterns and your geographical understanding. For example, houses have been built in an area with a medium risk of flooding. These might be new developments indicating the expansion of Newborough.

Use the data layers together with the base map to interpret the image. For example, the majority of houses in Newborough have been built in an area that is not at risk of flooding from rivers or the sea.

One advantage of GIS is that you can select the geographical information you want to see. These buttons allow the user to select different levels of risk of flooding.

(10) Layers of data

Figure 2 This satellite image of the Sperry Glacier in Montana has been enhanced with information to show how the area covered by the glacier has changed since 1966.

If precise data is used, the GIS map will be very accurate. This means correct measurements (e.g. the rate of glacial retreat) can be made.

Ground photos, aerial photos and satellite photos, along with data from visiting the glacier, were used to work out exactly how far the ice cover extended. This data was then put into GIS to map the lines.

When a GIS image has a scale, you can use the scale to measure the change. For example, the scale here shows the distance in kilometres that the glacier has retreated since 1966.

(5) Exam-style practice   Grades 4–6

Explain how GIS might be used to investigate how parts of a city have grown.   **[4 marks]**

 Made a start   **Feeling confident**   **Exam ready**

Calculations

You need to be able to calculate percentage increase and decrease and understand the use of percentiles, proportions and ratios.

Percentage increase and decrease

A percentage increase or decrease shows how much geographical data has changed. For example, you could calculate how much the width of a river channel increases as you travel downstream.

Calculating percentage increase

Use this method when something has grown bigger, so the first number (original number) is smaller than the second number (new number).

1 Find the increase by calculating the difference between the two numbers:

new number – original number = increase

2 Divide the increase by the original number and multiply the answer by 100:

$$\text{percentage increase} = \frac{\text{increase}}{\text{original number}} \times 100$$

Calculating percentage decrease

Use this method when the original number is bigger than the new number.

1 Find the decrease:

original number – new number = decrease

2 Divide the decrease by the original number and multiply the answer by 100:

$$\text{percentage decrease} = \frac{\text{decrease}}{\text{original number}} \times 100$$

 Key terms

- **Proportion**: the number or amount of a group or part of something when compared to the whole.
  - **Direct proportion**: when two values are in direct proportion, one increases as the other increases.
  - **Inverse proportion**: when two values are in inverse proportion, one increases as the other decreases. For example, one doubles as the other halves.
- **Ratio**: the relationship between two quantities
- **Magnitude**: how big something is
- **Frequency**: how often something happens
- **Percentile**: percentiles divide a list of numbers into percentages. If you are in the 60th percentile for height in your class, 60 per cent of the class are shorter than you. It is an indicator of how the data is spread around the median.
- **Quartiles**: the values that divide a list of numbers into quarters
- **Quintiles**: the values that divide a list of numbers into fifths

Calculating ratios

A ratio is a way to compare values. For example, if 6000 people died in a tropical cyclone out of a population of 12 million, you could express the ratio of the number of deaths to the number of people in the affected area. Simplify both sides to make the ratio more manageable.
6000:12 000 000 = 6:12 000 = 1:2000

Worked example Grades 3–6

Study **Figure 1**, which shows the population of London at different times in millions of people.

Figure 1

1951	1971	1991	2001	2011
8.1	7.4	6.8	7.1	8.1

(a) Calculate the percentage increase in London's population between 1991 and 2011. Give your answer to one decimal place. **[2 marks]**

Increase = 8.1 − 6.8 = 1.3
1.3 ÷ 6.8 × 100 = 19.1%

> Start by calculating 1% of the original number.

(b) London's population is projected to increase by 19.7% between 2011 and 2024. Calculate the projected population of London in 2024. **[2 marks]**

Population in 2011 = 8.1 million = 100%
1% of 8.1 = 0.081
Percentage increase = 19.7%
0.081 × 19.7 = 1.5957 ≈ 1.6 ◄
8.1 million + 1.6 million = 9.7 million

> If 1% is 0.081, then 19.7% is 19.7 × 0.081.

Exam-style practice Grades 4–6

Two quantities are in direct proportion when they increase or decrease in the same ratio.
9 litres of petrol costs £11.25. How much does 20 litres cost? **[1 mark]**

 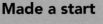

Statistical skills

In the exam, you could be expected to use appropriate measures of central tendency and spread to investigate relationships in data.

 Measures of central tendency

Measures of central tendency are also known as averages.

Calculating averages
- **Mean** – add all the values together and divide by the number of values. The mean can be affected by extreme values.
- **Median** – organise the values numerically from lowest to highest and take the middle value. If there are two middle values, the median is halfway between them. The median is not affected by extreme values.
- **Mode** – find the value that occurs most often. This can apply to data that are not numerical, such as colours.
- **Modal class** – if the data set is grouped into classes, the modal class is the most frequently occurring group of data in the data set.

 **Measures of spread**

Measures of spread show how the data are distributed, for instance the **interquartile range** shows how far values are spread from the median.

The **range** is calculated by subtracting the smallest value from the largest value. If the range is big, the spread of the data is large. Spread can be affected by extreme values.

To find the interquartile range you must work out the upper and lower quartiles. The IQR is the difference between these two values. The median is the central value of the IQR.

Lower quartile = $\frac{1}{4}$ $(n + 1)$th value

Upper quartile = $\frac{3}{4}$ $(n + 1)$th value

> n is the number of values in the data set.

IQR = upper quartile – lower quartile

 Worked example **Grade 4**

1 Calculate the interquartile range of this set of numbers. **[2 marks]**

1 12 15 19 20 24 28 34 37 47 50

Lower quartile = $\frac{1}{4}$ (11 + 1) = 3rd value

so the lower quartile is 15

Upper quartile = $\frac{3}{4}$ (11 + 1) = 9th value

so the upper quartile is 37

Interquartile range = 37 – 15 = 22

2 Study **Figure 1**, which shows data from a river investigation. Identify the modal class. **[1 mark]**

Size of stones (mm)	Number of stones collected
1–5	24
6–10	10
11–15	5
16–20	22
21–25	9

Figure 1

1–5 mm

 Calculating measures of central tendency and spread

Mean

$\frac{3 + 7 + 8 + 8 + 12 + 17 + 22}{7} = 11$

Median

3 7 8 8 12 17 22   Median

Mode

3 7 8 8 12 17 22   Mode

Modal class

	0–10	11–20	21–30
Frequency	4	2	1

Range

22 – 3 = 19

Interquartile range

17 – 7 = 10   Upper quartile / Lower quartile

 Practice **Grade 4**

The UK's population increased from approximately 55 million in 1970 to approximately 62 million in 2010. Calculate the percentage increase. **[2 marks]**

      Made a start **Feeling confident** **Exam ready**

Describing relationships in data

In the exam, you may also need to describe relationships between two sets of data and predict values based on a set of data.

⑤ Relationships in bivariate data

Bivariate data is data for two related variables.
Bivariate data is usually shown as a scattergraph.

The x axis is the **independent** variable.

The y axis is the **dependent** variable.

Figure 1 shows how scattergraph could be used to look at the relationship between GDP and literacy.

The points of the graph can be examined to see whether they form a pattern or relationship.

A line of best fit that runs through the middle of the points can be drawn to identify whether there is a:

- strong or weak **correlation** (strong – if the points are close to the line, or weak – if the points are further away from the line) or no correlation
- positive or negative correlation.

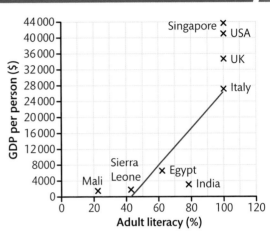

Figure 1 Scattergraph showing the relationship between GDP and literacy

⑤ Key term

Correlation relationship

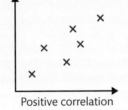
Positive correlation

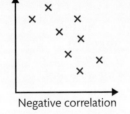
Negative correlation

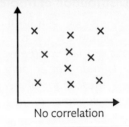
No correlation

② Interpolating and extrapolating trends

Interpolating and extrapolating trends in a data set allows you to predict a value for which data is not available.

- Interpolation is estimating an unknown value within a data set.
- Extrapolation is estimating an unknown value outside a data set.

You can estimate an unknown value by plotting the data you do have on a graph and then using the line of best fit to predict the unknown value. To extrapolate, extend the line of best fit beyond the first and last point. You can estimate the values by reading from the line of best fit. See page 93 for information on scattergraphs and lines of best fit.

Interpolation and extrapolation is particularly useful for predicting environmental conditions, such as rainfall, temperature or air pollution levels, at locations for which you have no data.

⑤ Worked example Grades 4–6

Study **Figure 1**, which is a scattergraph showing GDP per person and adult literacy. Describe the relationship between GDP per capita and adult literacy. **[2 marks]**

The graph shows a positive correlation, which means that as GDP per capita increases, adult literacy also increases.

② Exam-style practice Grades 4–6

Using **Figure 1**, explain **one** problem with using scattergraphs to show relationships between two sets of data. **[2 marks]**

Answers

Page 1 General atmospheric circulation
A Hadley cell

Page 2 Causes of climate change
Increased rates of deforestation reduce the amount of carbon dioxide (a greenhouse gas) that is removed from the atmosphere, which contributes to global warming. *You could also have mentioned: burning fossil fuels; agriculture; beef production/rice farming.*

Page 3 Climate change evidence
Global sea levels rose by about 14 cm in the last 100 years due to increased temperatures causing glaciers and ice sheets to melt. Sea level rise is also due to thermal expansion as warmer water takes up more space. *You could also have mentioned: thickness of sea ice; glaciers retreating; coral bleaching; or decrease in size of ice sheets.*

Page 4 Predicting climate change
There is a range of climate change projections produced by different scientists and computer models. These varying predictions lead to uncertainty about the extent of the change. *You could also have mentioned: the rate of future greenhouse gas emissions; or the rate of population increase.*

Page 5 Distribution of tropical cyclones
Tropical cyclones can only form in areas where the sea's surface temperature is at least 26.5 °C. *You could also have mentioned: latitude (between approximately 5° and 30° latitude); the amount of water vapour in the atmosphere; the location of areas of low pressure and storms joining together; or the Coriolis effect.*

Page 6 Causes and hazards of tropical cyclones
Warm ocean water (at least 26.5 °C) leads to warm air rising rapidly and water evaporating, causing thunderstorms. These converge, and an area of very low pressure forms. As the air rises, it starts to spin, accelerating in speed.

Page 7 Impacts of tropical cyclones
Bangladesh is located at the north-eastern end of the Bay of Bengal. The funnel shape of the coastline increases wind speeds and the height of storm surges. *You could also have mentioned: Bangladesh is low-lying, which makes it vulnerable to storm surges.*

Page 8 Preparing and responding
1. One way countries can prepare for tropical cyclones is by installing early warning systems such as the one in Bangladesh. These help to reduce the death toll by allowing people time to evacuate. *You could also have mentioned: building sea walls; or disseminating information from the Red Cross.*

2. Satellite images are useful in forecasting which areas tropical cyclones will affect, so people can make preparations to protect themselves and their property from the tropical storm.

Page 9 Examples of tropical cyclones
Developing countries have more challenges in preparing for tropical cyclones than developed countries that experience tropical cyclones of a similar magnitude. For example, Typhoon Haiyan hit the Philippines, a developing country, in 2013. Over 7000 people died and 1.9 million people were left homeless after the cyclone and its exceptionally high (7 m) storm surges. This could be seen as evidence that developing countries like the Philippines cannot prepare effectively for tropical cyclones. However, this would be a very unfair conclusion. The Philippines experiences around 20 tropical cyclones each year and Haiyan was its 25th in 2013. The reason Haiyan caused so much death and destruction compared to the other 24 tropical cyclones that year, was that it was one of the strongest tropical cyclones ever recorded anywhere in the world.

The Philippines weather agency, PAGASA, monitored the approach of Haiyan and warned of storm surges two days before it made landfall. Around 750 000 people were evacuated before Haiyan made landfall, which shows effective preparations were made. Unfortunately, Haiyan's extreme storm surges flooded evacuation centres even in areas that had never flooded before.

The Filipino government's preparations for Haiyan can be criticised. For example, they used a term for 'storm surge' that local people did not understand, so many people did not evacuate. Developed countries have more money for public awareness campaigns to ensure people understand such key information.

However, overall it is incorrect to say that developing countries cannot prepare effectively for tropical cyclone hazards. The Philippines has systems for dealing effectively with tropical cyclones, but Haiyan was such an extreme cyclone with which they were unable to cope.

Page 10 Earth's layered structure
The mantle is heated by radioactive decay in the Earth's core, creating convection currents. When the currents reach the solid rock of the crust, they start to move along the asthenosphere. The tectonic plates in the Earth's crust move along with them.

Page 11 Plate boundary types
At conservative plate boundaries, plates slide past each other. This means subduction and melting do not occur so magma is not produced.

Page 12 Tectonic hazards
Tectonic activity can cause a tsunami when an earthquake occurs at a convergent plate boundary. A huge amount of pressure is suddenly released and this displaces a very large volume of water at the epicentre of the earthquake, causing a tsunami. *You could also have mentioned: tectonic movement can trigger landslides into the ocean, displacing a large volume of water.*

Page 13 Impacts of earthquakes
It will be difficult to devise a *y*-axis scale that can accurately include such a wide range of numbers, from 2 to 175 827.

Page 14 Impacts of volcanoes

Developed countries can afford effective monitoring technology, which is less likely to be available in developing countries. This makes it possible to warn people about an imminent eruption, allowing them to evacuate. *You could also have mentioned: developed countries can afford more effective responses so people can be rescued; or there may be better insurance schemes so people can get money to repair or rebuild damaged property.*

Page 15 Managing earthquake hazards

B Long-term planning

Page 16 Managing volcano hazards

Volcanic eruption prediction is usually more effective in developed countries because they have money for monitoring technology. For example, before an eruption, seismometers can measure earth movements, and tiltmeters can measure the swelling of the ground. GPS satellites can measure changes in the shape of the volcano, and specialised instruments can measure changes in the gases the volcano releases. This data is fed into modelling software to predict how high the risk of eruption is, where on the volcano the eruption is likely to occur, and when it is likely to happen. Developing countries also have access to this technology. However, developed countries are likely to have more technology operating at the same time, a longer history of measurement of the same volcanoes, which helps with modelling, and more scientists with the training and experience to operate the technology and to interpret the results. All this makes volcanic eruption prediction more effective in developed countries than in developing countries.

Analysing data from past eruptions to produce risk maps identifies the areas at the highest risk. This allows governments to plan the best routes for evacuation in the event of an eruption, and set up exclusion areas, which prevent development in high risk areas. Developed countries are often much more able to stop people from living in areas that are high risk than developing countries, where many people need land, which means volcanic eruptions tend to have a greater impact.

Page 17 Development

A social measure of development, such as HDI, defines development as being more than just how economically developed a country is; it considers how developed a country's quality of life is by considering factors such as life expectancy and literacy rates.

Page 18 Levels of development

India's population structure shows that there is a high birth rate, as the the base of the pyramid is still wide – wider than both Malawi and the UK. There are a greater number of working age people (20–65), which indicates that healthcare in India has improved and the rate of infant mortality is low, with infants surviving into adulthood.

Page 19 Global inequalities

Inequality between countries causes economic migration, when people move from a country with fewer opportunities and lower pay to one that offers more opportunities and higher pay. Lack of healthcare, education opportunities and basic services encourage people to move to a more developed country where these are available. *You could also have mentioned: politics; or people move from countries with unstable or corrupt governments to live in safer countries.*

Page 20 Theories of development

Rostow maintained that countries pass through five stages of economic growth. They start off as traditional societies, where most people work on the land and live in rural areas. As infrastructure and machinery improve, farmers can sell their goods and make a profit, so trading and manufacturing increase.

Many developing countries are now entering the take-off stage as industry grows rapidly, and trade and communications increase.

Many emerging countries, like India and China, have passed through this stage and have entered the drive to maturity stage, where economic growth extends across all parts of the economy and old industries are replaced by new.

The developed countries of the world are in the stage of high mass consumption. As there is lots of wealth spread across the country, people can afford to buy lots of products, which creates demand for more industry and growth.

Page 21 Approaches to development

A Experts work with locals to identify their needs.

Page 22 Advantages and disadvantages

A A network of canals to irrigate 2 million hectares of farmland

Page 23 Emerging economy: India

India is affected by the monsoon, which brings a wet season to large parts of the country. The rain brought by the monsoon is vital for water supply and for farming, which requires land to be flooded for some of the time. However, heavy rain and strong winds can cause flooding and severe damage to land and property.

Page 24 India: Economic change and development

1. One area of rapid development was telecommunications. Many TNCs invested in call centres in India since wages were much lower than in other countries, even for well-educated English speakers. Globalisation has also facilitated growth in India's manufacturing sector, whose products are sold around the world.

2. Firstly, India's GDP has grown on a massive scale since 1970–71. All sectors of the economy have grown, but the tertiary sector has seen the largest increase. In 1970–71, primary industry contributed most to India's economy. By 2010–11, this had been overtaken by tertiary industry.

3. One reason why India's secondary industry has increased could be due to the Indian's government policy to open up its economy to FDI, which has allowed many TNCs to open up factories and manufacture goods in India.

Page 25 India: Impacts of development

$5498 \div 1395 = 3.94$

Goa's GDP per capita was 3.94 times higher than the mean.

Page 26 India and globalisation

When foreign companies (TNCs) invest in a developing country, local people who are employed by the TNC spend the money they earn in the developing country. This means local businesses and services have more trade, so the government receives more in taxes. It can invest the taxes in infrastructure such as new ports, power stations, broadband and railways, which increase economic development. *You could also have mentioned: the way TNC investment develops skills, which the labour force can then transfer to other industries in the country; or the way TNC investment can create multiplier effects as supplier industries develop to support the TNC's production.*

Page 27 Urbanisation trends

13 – 9.9 = 3.1

3.1/9.9 × 100 = 31.31%

Page 28 Growing cities

One characteristic of a declining city is declining quality of life. *You could also have mentioned: people in the city find it harder to get jobs; companies in the city reduce the number of people they employ; the city government receives less money in taxes; the city's economy slows/declines.*

Page 29 Different urban economies

One reason is that governments in developing countries may not enforce laws on working conditions, such as health and safety laws, and may not allow unions to improve conditions for workers.

Page 30 Changing cities

B Suburbanisation

Page 31 Megacity: Mumbai

For highly skilled global migrants, Mumbai offers world-class economic opportunities in IT and other high-tech industries. However, the majority of the 1000 people per day who migrate to Mumbai come from rural areas of India. They are attracted by the opportunities to earn money in Mumbai's informal sector.

Page 32 Mumbai: Opportunities and challenges

In Mumbai, the main form of slum settlement is chawls. Some chawls are in danger of collapsing because their landlords have not repaired them. *You could also have mentioned: squatter settlements in Mumbai are also overcrowded: in Dharavi shanty town, 1 million people live in an area of 1.5 km^2 and so there is a risk of disease spreading; one challenge is that the squatter settlements are built on land that often floods.*

Page 33 Mumbai: Sustainability

The SPARC community toilet block project is a bottom-up scheme in which the local community helps build toilet blocks. For a very cheap monthly fee, the community can use the toilets and they are maintained. This contributes to the city's sustainability by reducing the spread of disease and helping to prevent the dumping of human sewage in local streams and rivers, and onto wasteland.

Page 34 The UK's physical landscape

Most sedimentary rocks are formed when weathered and eroded rock is cemented together in horizontal layers.

Metamorphic rocks are a result of changes in temperature and pressure inside the Earth's crust.

Page 35 UK landscapes and rock groups

Granite upland landscapes *or* Limestone upland landscapes.

Page 36 Landscapes and human activity

The map in **Figure 1** showing Lincolnshire is more suitable for arable farming than the upland Cairngorms location shown in **Figure 2** for several reasons. The main reason is relief. The area of Lincolnshire in **Figure 1** is very flat, which makes it suitable for ploughing, sowing and harvesting. The area of the Cairngorms shown in **Figure 2** has very steep slopes, which is evident from how close together the contour lines are in the north-east. Steep slopes are very difficult to plough for crops. *You could also have mentioned: the location in **Figure 2** is heavily forested, which makes it unsuitable for arable farming.*

Page 37 Coastal erosion landforms

1. An arch, such as Durdle Door in Dorset, forms from erosion of a headland. The prevailing winds blow destructive waves towards the base of the headland. Erosion, such as hydraulic action, and weathering, such as freeze-thaw, creates pressure in the faults or cracks in the headland. Over time, the faults grow, and eventually they become a small cave. Continued erosional processes such as hydraulic action and collision of rock fragments (abrasion) cause the cave to deepen. Eventually the sea breaks through the back of the cave, forming an arch.

Continued erosion widens the arch. Eventually the top of the arch collapses, leaving a pinnacle of rock detached from the mainland, called a stack.

2. A discordant coastline is made up of alternating bands of hard and soft rock, which run at right angles to the sea, whereas on a concordant coastline, the geology runs parallel to the sea. On a discordant coastline, as the hard and soft rocks are exposed to wave action, the softer, weaker rock is eroded more easily to form bays, and the hard rock forms headlands. Coves, such as Lulworth Cove in Dorset, can form in weaknesses in the hard rock of a concordant coastline.

Page 38 Processes of coastal erosion

Destructive waves create more erosion as they are tall and have a short wavelength. This results in a weak swash and strong backwash, which takes sediments off the beach. Constructive waves are much shorter and have a longer wavelength. This results in a low-energy wave that deposits material on the beach.

Page 39 Mass movement and transportation

1. *Any one from:* sliding (the sudden movement of large volumes of material along an area of saturated soil); slumping (the mass movement of saturated permeable rock and soil on top of impermeable rock); or rock falls (the free-fall movement of rock fragments due to gravity).

2. Slumping can result in large sections of cliff collapsing onto the beach below. This can result in the loss of farmland and coastal properties and the destruction of stretches of coastal footpaths.

Page 40 Coastal deposition landforms

1. Low-energy constructive waves deposit sediment to form a low beach profile. Destructive waves erode sediment forming a steeper beach profile.

2. Figure 2 shows a sand bar, which may be submerged by rising sea levels in the future. The coastline could then retreat.

Page 41 Human activities in coastal landscapes
Is the height of the beach greater closer to the groynes? You would need to select two variables within the image to test – in this case, the height of the beach and proximity to the groynes.

Page 42 The changing Holderness coast
On the Holderness coastline, human activities include constructing coastal defences at the village of Mappleton. This has reduced the rate of coastal erosion at this location, but may have increased erosion of the cliffs at Aldborough, which is south of Mappleton.

Page 43 Coastal flooding
Any two from: Roads and railways could be washed away or damaged, especially if bridges are damaged or tunnels flooded. Industries located at the coastline, such as power plants, sewage works or oil refineries, might have to shut down because of damage. Houses and businesses could become uninhabitable because of flooding or increased erosion to cliffs that they are located on or near. There would be an increased risk of mass movement, because of erosion to cliff bases or saturation of cliffs caused by flooding. This could make human activity in some areas very dangerous.

Page 44 Coastal management options
Hornsea has been protected by groynes to build up the beach with sediment that has been trapped by longshore drift. **Figure 4** shows that there is housing, a caravan park and a car park close to the shore, which needs to be protected from coastal erosion. Building up the beach also provides a good beach for use by tourists who may be visiting the nearby caravan park.

Page 45 River landscapes
In the upper course of a river, the river's load consists of large and angular sediment as the river does not have much energy or discharge, so erosion is limited. In the middle and lower course, discharge is increased, producing more energy so the load becomes more rounded and smaller due to attrition and abrasion.

Page 46 The course of the River Severn
1. Meander

2. The contours at the sides of the river are widely spaced, indicating that the land is flat and has formed a floodplain.

Page 47 River processes
1. *Any one from:* traction, suspension, solution or saltation.

2. Hydraulic action and abrasion increase the width and depth (cross-sectional area) of the river channel downstream. Hydraulic action is the repeated force of the water on the river beds and bank, which traps air in cracks. This increases pressure and weakens the bed and banks, widening and deepening the river channel. Abrasion is the action of rock fragments carried by the river scraping against the banks and bed which causes them to wear down.

Page 48 River erosion landforms
Less resistant rock is eroded by the hydraulic action and abrasion of a waterfall, leading to the collapse of more resistant rock that is unsupported. As a waterfall retreats upstream, this repeated cycle will form a steep-sided gorge.

Page 49 River erosion and deposition landforms
Meanders are generally found in the middle course of a river. The fast-flowing current moves quickly on the outside of the bend and causes lateral erosion and hydraulic action as the force of the water against the bed and the banks begins to wear them away. On the inside of the bend, the flow is slower due to greater friction so sand and shingle are deposited. Over time, this forms a slip-off slope.

Page 50 Storm hydrographs
1. 6 hours *(reading from the right-hand side of the bar, from 8 p.m. to 2 a.m.)*

2. Heavy precipitation causes land to become saturated quickly, increasing surface runoff and the volume of water reaching the river, which increases the peak discharge. Lighter precipitation causes a longer lag time as the precipitation infiltrates into the soil, reducing surface runoff and producing a lower peak discharge.

Page 51 Factors affecting storm hydrographs
Deforestation leaves soil bare, which increases surface runoff and leads to a flashy hydrograph. In areas with heavy vegetation, leaves on trees and plants intercept rainfall, and plant roots help infiltration, both of which reduces surface runoff, so water takes longer to reach the river.

Page 52 River flooding risks
Physical processes that contributed to flooding on the River Cocker in Cumbria include rainfall, as Cumbria is a mountainous area in the north-west of England that experiences a high average rainfall of over 2000 mm per year. The mountainous terrain caused increased surface runoff from the steep slopes, so a large volume of water reached the river, causing flooding. Another physical process that contributed to flooding of the River Cocker was the intense period of rainfall caused by Storm Desmond in 2015, during which over 340 mm rainfall fell in 24 hours.

Page 53 Managing flood risk
Soft engineering methods such as river restoration (reintroduction of meanders and wetland areas) are generally cheaper than hard engineering methods.

Page 54 The UK's human landscape
Figure 3 shows a younger population for London with a higher percentage of people under 35. Somerset has a broader top to its pyramid, showing a higher percentage of people over 40. **Figure 3** shows equal numbers of male and female, while there are more women than men in the older age groups in Somerset. *You could also have mentioned: more 0–4 year olds are shown in **Figure 3** than in **Figure 4**.*

Page 55 Reducing differences
New developments (e.g. HS2) reduce the need to increase capacity on the rail network, which is overcrowded. Improvements to connectivity between different areas of the UK boost economic growth and reduce regional disparity.

Page 56 Migration and the UK

Your reasons could include: to find work by moving from an area of higher unemployment to one where there are more jobs; to retire, for example by moving to a popular retirement area such as the south coast, which has warmer average temperatures than the north; to go to university; or to move to an area with more affordable house prices.

Page 57 Economic change in the UK

Cities, such as London and Manchester, have experienced economic growth in recent years because new tertiary and quaternary industries have developed in these urban areas. Industries, such as banking and web design, have located and grown up in these cities because they have large universities, which are able to provide the skilled workforce required for knowledge-based service industries.

Page 58 Investing in the UK

Nearly half of all FDI in the UK is in financial services. London is a global financial centre, which has attracted FDI. The fall in the value of sterling following the Brexit referendum has made investing in the UK cheaper for foreign TNCs.

Page 59 A major UK city: London

In the centre (CBD) of London the air quality is poor because of the high level of vehicles that travel through and within it. As you move out towards the suburbs and urban-rural fringe, there are more green spaces, less traffic and air pollution.

Page 60 Population changes

1. The largest concentrations of the ethnic population are found to the north of the river Thames in the more central areas. The further away from the centre of London, the lower the amount of the ethnic population. The outer areas have a very low ethnic population, less than 20% of the population living there is from ethnic groups.

2. Much of the ethnic population may be made up of migrants who have moved to London for employment. They may have settled close to the centre where there are more job opportunities.

Many migrants move into the inner city, where there is high density housing, which is often cheaper to rent.

Page 61 Unequal London

Hackney is a more deprived area in the inner city of London. There is a much greater level of unemployment. This could be due to deindustrialisation and the loss of jobs in the inner cities. Fewer people in Hackney work in higher paid jobs as managers and professionals, compared to Richmond. This could be because GCSE attainment is lower in Hackney than Richmond. This might mean that people in Hackney earn lower wages, which may be a reason why a much greater number of children are entitled to free school meals.

Page 62 Growth and regeneration

One advantage of the regeneration in Stratford in East London is that the new stadium and Westfield shopping centre have attracted more visitors to the area, who spend money and boost the local economy.

One disadvantage is that the newer high-class housing is too expensive for local people, who, as a result, have had to move out of the area.

Page 63 Sustainable London

In London, the congestion charge was introduced, which charges most vehicles to enter central parts of London. This has reduced the number of cars on the roads and the amount of CO_2 emissions in the atmosphere. At the same time, London introduced a bicycle rental scheme, which made it easy to rent a bicycle for the day to travel around central London. Bicycles do not emit any harmful gases into the atmosphere and therefore make London's air cleaner.

Page 64 Challenges facing rural areas

Figure 1 shows that Effingham Common is currently an open green space covered in grass. The environmental impacts of development might include loss of wildlife habitats resulting in a reduction in biodiversity. *You could also have mentioned: traffic congestion on local roads as people commute from Effingham Common to take their children to school.*

Page 65 Exam skills: Human geography enquiries

Location B looks like it may be a private gated area that students may not have been able to access. There may not have been as many people around in location B on a Thursday afternoon to answer the questionnaire during working hours. The people around location B may not live in the area, but may just work in the offices there. Location A may be a less safe area for students as there are alleyways.

Page 66 Exam skills: Human geography data collection

A traffic count is an example of a quantitative method. A traffic count is fairly accurate because it involves counting the actual number of cars and vehicles passing a certain point over a certain period of time.

Page 67 Exam skills: Presenting human geography data

The annotated diagram shows a traffic count conducted in Grasmere in June. The proportional arrows show the volume of traffic at 2pm on a Wednesday afternoon. The wider the base of the arrow, the higher the volume of traffic. The traffic moving south toward Ambleside was greater than the traffic going north to Keswick. This could be because Ambleside has more services and attractions, so more visitors and locals choose to travel to Ambleside.

Page 68 Exam skills: Physical geography enquiries

Your answer will depend on whether you did your fieldwork in a river or coastal environment.

Rivers – you may have referred to the Bradshaw model, which explains the theory of how river characteristics change as the river flows through its long course. As a result, you may have tested how either width, depth and discharge increase as a river flows downstream or how the load of the river decreases and becomes more rounded further downstream.

Coasts – you may have referred back to the topic on coastal defences and how groynes trap sediment being transported by longshore drift. You may therefore have tested whether the beach gradient was steeper and sediment build-up was greater on the side of the groyne facing the direction of the prevailing wind.

Page 69 Exam skills: Physical geography data collection

You need to assess at least two types of secondary data use. For rivers, you should have used an Environment Agency Flood Risk Map and one other secondary source; for coasts, you should have used a geology map and one other secondary source, such as geology maps, OS maps, newspaper articles, websites, census data.

The Environment Agency Flood Risk Map would show the areas that are most at risk from flooding, based on previous floods and landscape features. They are very reliable sources that are useful to identify areas that have flooded or are at risk. However, they may not be updated regularly and if something changes, such as a new car park and/or a bridge is built, they may have out-of-date information.

Geology maps and OS maps are useful at identifying contrasting areas and identifying land use and relief, but they often don't contain the smaller details, so visits to the site and the collection of primary data is necessary to investigate the area fully.

Page 70 Exam skills: Presenting physical geography data

Student's own answer

Page 71 Exam skills: Analysis, conclusion and evaluation

This will depend on the type of study you did. If you studied how quality of life is different between two areas, you might conclude that quality of life is better in one of those areas. You may have conducted an environmental quality survey in each area and judged one area to have a better-quality environment, with more green spaces and less litter. This type of survey, however, is very subjective as it is based on a person's opinion and is therefore not always reliable. If you sampled a number of people in each area to conduct a questionnaire about the area, the results could show that people in one area are happier with the environment than in the other. It would be important to consider when and where you conducted the questionnaires, because if this was done on a weekday during the day, then many people are at work or school, so the sample is not fully representative and could affect the results and conclusions made.

Page 72 Biomes and the biosphere

Deforestation reduces the biomass store, which is the main store of nutrients. This will reduce the supply of nutrients to the soil store, which will become much smaller.

Page 73 A life-support system

Any one of the following: genetic engineering of crops, making them resistant to diseases; development of improved fertilisers that make crops grow faster and produce higher yields; mechanisation of farming, which means that seeds are planted efficiently and accurately, which improves yields; development of new farming areas such as the Great Plains of the USA; refrigeration and freezing, which means food can be transported long distances between countries and stored until it is needed.

Page 74 Tropical rainforest characteristics

The rainforest does not have a winter season when plants stop using nutrients, so trees are constantly taking up nutrients resulting in soils that are low in nutrients. High levels of precipitation mean that any remaining nutrients are leached downwards, so the soils are nutrient poor. *You could also have mentioned: nutrients do not have a chance to build up in the tropical rainforest soil because of leaching. There is heavy rain in rainforests most days, which leaches nutrients out of the top layers of the soil.*

Page 75 Threats to tropical rainforest

A reduction in the amount of insect life in the litter layer would cause a reduction in the number of animals who live off of the insects, such as tenrecs and giant anteaters.

Page 76 Sustainable rainforests

1. A possible reason is a major increase during those years in the price of a commercial crop such as soybeans, palm oil or beef. Big price increases encourage commercial farmers to clear rainforest land in order to expand their production rapidly and make a lot more money from a much larger harvest of that product. *You could also have mentioned: one reason could be a change from a government that was strict about rainforest protection to one that did not believe rainforest protection should continue.*

2. Prices of commercial crops (such as soybeans) have increased, which encourages the clearance of rainforests to increase production and profit. *You could also have mentioned: population growth drives urbanisation, which requires land for building.*

Page 77 Taiga forest characteristics

Conifers are adapted to the taiga forest climate because they are evergreen, so they do not drop their leaves in autumn. Therefore, they do not need to grow new leaves each spring, which takes a lot of energy. They are also ready to start photosynthesising in spring. *You could also have mentioned: conifers are also often cone-shaped, with branches sloping downwards. This makes snow slide off them, which helps to prevent them being damaged by the weight of snow in winter.*

Page 78 Threats to taiga forest

The taiga is warming and experiencing shorter, less extremely cold winters so pests that were not able to survive, because of the long winter periods of extreme cold, can now not only survive but also spread.

Page 79 Protecting the taiga forest

Sustainable forest management is a long-term approach because of the length of time it takes for taiga trees to grow – some tree species can grow to over 300 years old. Logged areas are replanted with a mix of taiga tree species, which helps to maintain biodiversity. Newly planted areas are cleared of dead wood to reduce the risk of forest fires killing the young trees. After 40 years, the trees are not all logged. Instead, only some of the weaker trees are removed for timber, leaving plenty to reach their maximum size. These are not cut down for 120 years after they were planted. When they are cut down, replanting takes place again.

Page 80 Energy impacts

Using renewable resources does not produce carbon dioxide. If renewable resources are used instead of carbon-dioxide producing fossil fuels, carbon emissions will be reduced.

Page 81 Distribution of energy

A reliance on traditional fuel sources is likely to result in lower energy use per capita than a reliance on electricity produced from nuclear energy or by burning fossil fuels in power stations.

Page 82 Oil and the economy

There may have been a sudden increase in oil supply, perhaps from the discovery of a major new oilfield. A lot more oil on the market would reduce the price of oil. *You could also have mentioned: a sudden drop in demand for oil. This could happen if there was a major recession – if people stopped buying as many products, then factories would reduce production of these products. This would reduce the amount of oil needed for production and for the transportation networks that take the manufactured products to market.*

Page 83 Conventional and unconventional oil and gas

Environmental costs could include deforestation from clearing forests that grow over the tar sands area. This is an environmental cost because of loss of habitat and loss of a carbon store of greenhouse gases. *You could also have mentioned: heating the sand to remove the bitumen and processing the bitumen into oil involves a lot of energy, which releases greenhouse gases and contributes to the environmental costs of climate change. Moving the oil from the mining and processing location to where it will be used could also risk oil spills and oil leaks. This would damage local ecosystems as oil is highly polluting and difficult to remove, especially from the fragile polar or taiga ecosystems where tar sands are often found.*

Page 84 Reducing fossil fuel reliance

The benefits of hydroelectric power include the fact that it is not a finite resource, so it will never run out. It also does not cause air pollution or emit greenhouse gases. The costs of hydroelectric power include the fact that it can flood very large areas, which can destroy wildlife habitats and result in the displacement of people. *You could also have mentioned: it can disrupt fish migration; it can harm river ecosystems; there is a finite number of suitable HEP sites.*

Page 85 Attitudes to energy futures

TNCs want to reduce production costs to make as much profit as possible. Since fossil fuels are usually cheaper than renewable energy, TNCs might prefer non-renewable energy sources, which are less sustainable. Environmentalists are often critical of TNCs, and may persuade governments to increase taxes or introduce fines for companies that do not use sustainable energy sources. TNCs may therefore move production to countries without these laws.

Page 86 Exam skills: Geographical issues

It will create more than 100 jobs, which would benefit people in the surrounding area who are looking for work. *You could also have mentioned: it provides coal for use in power stations which generate electricity for homes and businesses in the UK.*

Page 87 Making a geographical decision

Student's own answer

Page 88 Working with maps and atlases

The majority of earthquakes occur along plate boundaries, for example around the edge of the Pacific plate and a linear north-south pattern along the western edge of the South American plate. Few earthquakes are located away from plate boundaries and in the centre of landmasses.

Page 89 Coordinates, scale and distance

(a) 5724

(b) 568247

(c) 1.5 km

Page 90 Cross sections and contours

203 m above sea level

Page 91 Settlement site, situation and shape

Hutton Conyers village is surrounded by fields, so it is located in a rural farming area. It is situated along a road, which runs roughly north to south, and near to what appears to be a river or canal, which is located to the east of the settlement.

Page 92 Sketch maps and annotations

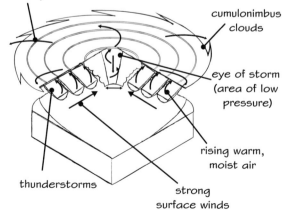

Page 93 Graphs and charts

1. Bar chart

2. Positive correlation

3. Line chart; histogram

Page 94 Maps and pyramids

3.3 million

Page 95 Using photos

Sediment has built up on one side of the groyne. Sediment moves along the beach in the direction of longshore drift, so this supports the student's annotation.

Page 96 Interpreting patterns from GIS

Satellite images, aerial photos and data from maps from different periods could be used to identify and measure urban sprawl over time. Data from these images could be mapped onto GIS layers, which could then be compared to see how the city has grown.

Page 97 Calculations

If 9 litres costs £11.25 then 1 litre costs £1.25, so 20 litres costs £25.00.

Page 98 Statistical skills

$62 - 55 = 7$

$\frac{7}{55} \times 100 = 13\%$

Page 99 Describing relationships in data

Although a line of best fit can be drawn which goes through or close to many of the points on the graph, there are some anomalies. For example, Singapore has the highest GDP per capita of all the countries but has a lower adult literacy rate than the UK and Italy. Scattergraphs do not account for anomalies.

Notes

Notes

Notes

Published by BBC Active, an imprint of Educational Publishers LLP, part of the Pearson Education Group, 80 Strand, London, WC2R 0RL.

www.pearsonschools.co.uk/BBCBitesize
© Educational Publishers LLP 2020
BBC logo © BBC 1996. BBC and BBC Active are trademarks of the British Broadcasting Corporation.

Typeset and illustrated by Newgen KnowledgeWorks Pvt. Ltd., Chennai, India

Editorial and project management services by Newgen Publishing UK

Cover design by Andrew Magee & Pearson Education Limited 2020

Cover illustration by Darren Lingard / Oxford Designers & Illustrators

The right of Rob Bircher to be identified as author of this work has been asserted by him in accordance with the Copyright, Designs and Patents Act 1988.

First published 2020

23 22 21 20
10 9 8 7 6 5 4 3 2 1

British Library Cataloguing in Publication Data

A catalogue record for this book is available from the British Library

ISBN 978 1 406 68600 5

Printed and bound in Slovakia by Neografia

The Publisher's policy is to use paper manufactured from sustainable forests.

Acknowledgements

Content written by Mike Chiles is included.

Text Credits:

P iii, 1-99: BBC; **P iii, 19**: United Nations Human Development Reports, United Nations Human Development Programme. Available under a CC-BY 3.0 IGO licence; **P iv:** Annual Carbon Emissions from Deforestation in the Amazon Basin between 2000 and 2010. PLoS One. 2015; 10(5), © Song et al Licensed under Creative Commons CC-BY; **P 3:** Global Surface Temperature, https://www.metoffice.gov.uk/research/monitoring/climate/surface-temperature

Met Office, © Crown Copyright. Contains public sector information licensed under the Open Government Licence v3.0; **P 17:** Table 1. Human Development Index and its components, Human Development Reports, United Nations Development Programme Available under a CC-BY 3.0 IGO licence; **P 18:** The World Fact Book, Central Intelligence Agency; **P 24:** Data from Government of India. Available under the Government Open Data License; **P 27:** World Urbanization Prospects: The 2014 Revision, (ST/ESA/SER.A/366), © United Nations, Department of Economic and Social Affairs, Population Division (2015); **P 34:** Colour-in geology map of the UK and Ireland, © British Geological Survey. Contains public sector information licensed under the Open Government Licence v3.0; **P 42:** Coastal Erosion Rates - Holderness Coastline, East Riding of Yorkshire Council. Contains public sector information licensed under the Open Government Licence v3.0; **P 43:** Data from Learn more about flood risk © Crown Copyright. Contains public sector information licensed under the Open Government Licence v3.0; **P 54:** 2011 Census, © Crown/Office for National Statistics. Contains public sector information licensed under the Open Government Licence v3.0; **P 54:** Subnational population projections for England: 2014-based, © Crown/Office for National Statistic Contains public sector information licensed under the Open Government Licence v3.0; **P 56:** © Crown/Office for National Statistics. Contains public sector information licensed under the Open Government Licence v3.0; **P 58:** UK foreign direct investment, trends and analysis: January 2018, © Crown/Office for National Statistic. Contains public sector information licensed under the Open Government Licence v3.0; **P 60:** London Data Store: London Borough Profiles and Atlas Greater London Authority (GLA). Contains public sector information licensed under the Open Government Licence v2.0; **P 60:** Measuring diversity: The London effect. Sep 16th 2013 (c) The Economist Newspaper Limited. Used with Permission; **P 61:** Summary Report of the 2015 Index of Multiple Deprivation, Barnet Council. Contains public sector information licensed under the Open Government Licence v2.0; **P 61:** London Borough Profiles and Atlas, © Greater London Authority. Contains public sector information licensed under the Open Government Licence v2.0; **P 76:** Annual Carbon Emissions from Deforestation in the Amazon Basin between 2000 and 2010, PLoS One. 2015, 10(5), (c) Song et al. Licensed under Creative Commons CC-BY; **P 81:** Energy use (kg of oil equivalent per capita), © The World Bank; **P 82:** Oil Consumption by Region. Statistical Review of World Energy 2017, 18 (2017) BP plc; **P 82:** Prices, Sales Volumes & Stocks by State, U.S. Energy Information Administration , U.S. Department of Energy; **P 85:** © Centre for Automotive Management (2018); P 88: © Istituto Nazionale di Statistica (2011)